Inside the
Gretsch Guitar
Factory

1957/1970

DAN DUFFY

Order this book online at www.trafford.com
or email orders@trafford.com

Most Trafford titles are also available at major online book retailers.

Print information available on the last page.

ISBN: 978-1-4120-6823-9 (sc)

Trafford rev. 08/10/2018

North America & international
toll-free: 1 888 232 4444 (USA & Canada)
fax: 812 355 4082

MY NAME IS DAN DUFFY AND I'M A GUITAR PLAYER. I WAS HIRED BY THE GRETSCH GUITAR COMPANY IN 1957 TO INSPECT AND PLAY EVERY GUITAR BEFORE IT LEFT THE FACTORY. IN THE PAST FEW YEARS I HAVE BEEN INTERVIEWED BY PEOPLE WRITING BOOKS ON GRETSCH GUITARS PRODUCED IN THE YEARS I WORKED THERE 1957 / 1970. NOW THESE GUITARS ARE IN A PRICE BRACKET THAT AMAZES ME.

I SIGNED ALL THOSE GREEN O.K. CARDS THAT HUNG ON THE HEADPIECE OF THE GUITAR. IN THE SIXTIES. WHEN THE PRODUCTION INCREASED BECAUSE OF THE DEMAND WE HIRED FRED RODRIGUEZ TO ASSIST ME. VARIOUS INSPECTION POINTS WERE SET UP THROUGHOUT THE FACTORY. FOR EXAMPLE, BEFORE THE GUITAR WAS SPRAYED WITH A LACQUER FINISH, IT WAS INSPECTED FOR ANY FLAWS IN THE WOOD THAT WERE NOT SANDED OUT. WHEN THE GUITAR WAS READY FOR THE ASSEMBLY DEPARTMENT IT WAS LOOKED AT AGAIN. ALL PARTS OF THE GUITAR SUCH AS THE NECKS, WERE CHECKED TO SEE IF THEY WERE STRAIGHT AND THE FRETS WERE PUT IN PROPERLY BEFORE THE NECK WAS FITTED TO THE BODY.

WHEN I STARTED THERE THE FACTORY WAS MAKING TEN

OR TWELVE GUITARS A DAY. DURING THE MIDDLE SIXTIES IT WAS
AROUND SEVENTY FIVE.

THE OLD SAYING "HASTE MAKES WASTE" DID NOT APPLY IN
THIS CASE. EVERYONE WORKED THEIR BUTT OFF TO MEET THE
DEMAND AND KEEP THE QUALITY AT AN ACCEPTABLE STANDARD.
BY THE WAY THAT WAS MY TITLE "QUALITY CONTROLLER"

WHEN I APPLIED FOR THE POSITION I REALLY DIDN'T KNOW
WHAT IT WAS ABOUT. SAL SALVADOR RECOMMENDED ME. HE
ENDORSED THE JAZZ GUITAR 6199 CONVERTIBLE, A WIDE BODY
ACOUSTIC GUITAR, WITH A FLOATING PICKUP ATTACHED TO THE
PICKGUARD. HE TOLD ME THAT THE GRETSCH COMPANY WAS LOOK-
ING FOR SOMEONE TO TUNE UP THE GUITARS. AT THAT TIME I WAS
WORKING IN AN OFFICE DURING THE DAY AND PLAYING AT LEAST
THREE NIGHTS A WEEK WITH MY BAND. I WANTED TO CHANGE MY
DAY JOB BECAUSE I WAS TIRED OF WAITING ON PROMISES THAT
NEVER HAPPENED, EVERYONE KNOWS WHAT THAT'S LIKE.

MY FIRST INTERVIEW FOR THE JOB WAS WITH PHIL GRANT
THE VICE PRESIDENT. HE ASKED ME ABOUT MY EDUCATION AND
PAST JOB EXPERIENCE. I GUESS HE TOOK IT FOR GRANTED THAT I
PLAYED THE GUITAR BECAUSE HE NEVER ASKED ME ABOUT IT. I RE-
MEMBER PRACTICING EVERY SPARE MINUTE I HAD, PRIOR TO THE
INTERVIEW TO MAKE A GOOD IMPRESSION. I HAD A COUPLE MORE
INTERVIEWS AFTER THAT AND NO ONE EVER ASKED ME TO PLAY.
I COULDN'T BELIEVE IT. LATER AFTER I WORKED THERE AWHILE I
ASKED JIMMY WEBSTER ABOUT THE FACT THAT NO ONE ASKED
ME TO PLAY. HE TOLD ME THAT SAL SALVADOR SAID I WAS A GOOD
PLAYER, AND THAT WAS GOOD ENOUGH FOR THEM. HE ALSO TOLD

ME THAT THEY NEEDED A PERSON WHO COULD HANDLE PRES-
SURE. IT WASN'T LONG BEFORE I KNEW WHAT HE MEANT. EVERY
TIME I SIGNED MY NAME TO THAT "O.K." CARD I ASSUMED THE RE-
SPONSIBILITY FOR THE GUITAR. I HAD TO TEACH MYSELF WHAT
EVERY ONE CALLED "COMMERCIALLY ACCEPTABLE." MY NUMBER
ONE PRIORITY FOR THE GUITAR WAS IT HAD TO PLAY EXTREMELY
WELL.

GETTING BACK TO MY INTERVIEW WITH PHIL GRANT, EVERY
THING WENT WELL AND HE TOLD I HAD TO SEE JIMMY WEBSTER
NEXT. HE MADE AN APPOINTMENT FOR ME THE FOLLOWING WEEK.
JIMMY WAS A VERY GOOD GUITAR PLAYER. HE WOULD DEMON-
STRATE THE GUITARS AT THE MUSIC SHOWS. HE USED A METHOD
OF PLAYING CALLED "THE TOUCH SYSTEM" HE WAS ALSO RESPON-
SIBLE FOR ALL THOSE GADGETS ON THE GUITARS. SOME WERE
VERY GOOD AND SOME WERE DUBIOUS. A PERFECT EXAMPLE OF
DUBIOUS WAS THE "TONE TWISTER" A SMALL METAL PIECE THAT
ATTACHED TO THE GUITAR BETWEEN THE BRIDGE AND THE TAIL-
PIECE. IT WAS SUPPOSED TO ACT LIKE A MINI VIBRATO. IT DIDN'T. IT
WAS INSTALLED ON SOME OF THE GUITARS AND TO MY AMAZEMENT
ORDERS CAME IN FOR THE "TONE TWISTER" . I ASKED THE MAN-
AGER OF ONE OF THE STORES ABOUT THIS AND HE TOLD ME THAT
SOME OF HIS CUSTOMERS LIKE THE WAY IT LOOKS ON THE GUI-
TAR, HE SAID THE MORE GADGETS, KNOBS AND SWITCHES ON THE
GUITARS THE BETTER. THE SALES OF THE TONE TWISTER EVENTU-
ALLY TWISTED ITS WAY INTO OBLIVION. JIMMY WAS RIGHT AGAIN,
"JUST MAKE IT AND THE SALES WILL COME" WAS HIS MOTTO.

THE STORY OF "THE PADDED BACK" . JIMMY CAME UP WITH

THE IDEA OF A "STEREO" GUITAR. THE WIRE HARNESS WAS VERY INTRICATE AND BULKY. IN ORDER TO INSTALL IT INTO THE GUITAR A FOUR OR FIVE INCH HOLE HAD TO BE CUT INTO THE BACK OF THE GUITAR. TO COVER THE HOLE A PAD WAS MADE. IT HAD SNAPS ON IT AND IT SNAPPED ONTO THE BACK OF THE GUITAR. THE "WHITE FALCON" STEREO GUITAR WAS INTRODUCED WITH THIS. A TRULY BEAUTIFUL GUITAR WITH A TRUE STEREO SOUND. JIMMY USED THIS GUITAR IN HIS DEMONSTRATIONS AND IT SOUNDED GREAT. CALLS CAME INTO THE FACTORY WITH REQUESTS TO HAVE THE PADDED BACK INSTALLED ON GUITARS THAT WERE JUST PUR-CHASED. ONCE AGAIN I WAS AMAZED. WHO WOULD WANT THIS THING ON THE BACK OF THEIR GUITAR? I KNOW I DIDN'T.

THEN THE PADDED BACK WENT ONE STEP FURTHER. "THE PADDED GUITAR" , OH GOD, WHAT NEXT. THIS THING LOOKED LIKE A GUITAR WITH A SKI JACKET ON. THIS GUITAR WAS NEVER PUT INTO PRODUCTION.

THE NEXT THING THAT REALLY GOT TO ME WAS THE TUN-ING FORK BRIDGE. THIS WILL BE A LITTLE HARD TO EXPLAIN. THE BRIDGE WAS MADE WITH THREE GOLD PLATED STEEL ROUND BARS.THE MIDDLE BAR WAS ABOUT THREE TIMES THICKER THAN THE OTHER TWO. IT HAD A TUNING FORK SCREWED INTO IT. A HOLE WAS MADE IN THE TOP OF THE GUITAR TO RECEIVE THE TUNING FORK. A SPACER BRIDGE WAS PLACED BEHIND IT. THIS DEVICE ACTUALLY MADE THE GUITAR SUSTAIN MORE, BUT CHANGING THE STRINGS WAS THE BIG PROBLEM. THE STRINGS CAME THROUGH THE TAILPIECE OVER THE SPACER BRIDGE OVER THE FIRST BAR OF THE TUNING FORK UNIT UNDER THE MIDDLE BAR THEN UP AND

OVER THE THIRD BAR THEN UP TO THE TUNING MACHINES. WHEN YOU STARTED TUNING THE STRINGS UP THE UNIT STARTED TWISTING. IT TOOK FOREVER TO CHANGE THE STRINGS. WHEN EVER A RACK OF TEN OR TWENTY OF THESE GUITARS WAS OUTSIDE MY TESTING BOOTH WAITING FOR ME TO TEST, INSPECT, AND SET THE INTONATION I CALLED FRED TO HELP ME. FRED HAD A LOT MORE PATIENCE THAN I DID, OR THAT'S THE IMPRESSION HE GAVE. FRED BECAME MY BEST FRIEND FOR LIFE.TO THIS DAY WE GET TOGETHER.WE STILL TALK ABOUT THE YEARS WE SPENT AT THE GRETSCH FACTORY. MY OTHER BEST FRIEND WAS FELIX PREVETE HIS NICKNAME WAS RED.

HE PASSED AWAY RECENTLY. RED STARTED WORKING AT GRETSCH WHEN HE WAS EIGHTEEN YEARS OLD. HE KNEW EVERY OPERATION IN THE FACTORY, HE BECAME THE FOREMAN OF THE ASSEMBLY DEPARTMENT. ON OCCASION FRED, RED AND MYSELF WOULD GO TO THE LOCAL BAR AND PLAY POOL OR SHUFFLE BOARD, HAVE A FEW BEERS AND TALK ABOUT GUITARS. I WAS ABOUT THIRTY YEARS OLD THEN AND I WAS TRULY IN GUITAR HEAVEN. UP UNTIL RED DIED, HE AND FRED WOULD COME TO LONG ISLAND TO SEE ME. RED STILL LIVED IN BROOKLYN AND FRED LIVES IN THE BRONX. WE WOULD GO TO THE LOCAL MARINA, CAST OUR FISHING LINES IN THE WATER, SIT BACK AND TALK ABOUT THE BEST YEARS OF OUR LIVES, WORKING AT GRETSCH GUITARS. FRED GRETSCH JR. WAS VERY FORTUNATE TO BE SURROUNDED BY SUCH DEDICATED PEOPLE. EVERYONE WHO WORKED THERE DID HIS OR HER BEST.

MY THIRD INTERVIEW WAS WITH HAROLD WOODS THE FAC-

TORY MANAGER AND HIS ASSISTANT BILL HAGNER WHO LATER BE-
CAME THE MANAGER AFTER HAROLD WOODS DEATH. THEY ASKED
ME THE SAME QUESTIONS, PAST WORK EXPERIENCE AND EDUCA-
TION. I ATTENDED THE SAME SCHOOLS AS BILL HAGNER SO THAT
WAS ANOTHER ONE FOR MY SIDE. EVENTUALLY THEY TOLD ME I
HAD THE JOB.THIS WAS THE BEGINNING OF MY CAREER IN THE
MUSIC BUSINESS. THIRTEEN YEARS WITH GRETSCH, SEVEN YEARS
WITH UNICORD, INC. AS GUITAR SERVICE MANAGER, THIRTEEN
YEARS AS GENERAL MANAGER OF VINCI GUITAR STRINGS AND
FINALLY FIVE YEARS AS PRESIDENT OF D'AQUISTO STRINGS OF
WHICH I HAVE A SMALL PERCENTAGE OF. I NEVER GOT A DIME OUT
OF IT SINCE I RETIRED. ALL THESE ARE STORIES IN THEMSELVES.

MY TOUR OF THE FACTORY WITH BILL HAGNER WAS GREAT.
HAVING BEEN GUITAR CRAZY SINCE I WAS ABOUT TWELVE YEARS
OLD I WAS ALL EYES. THE WOODSHOP WAS WHERE THEY ACTU-
ALLY MAKE THE GUITAR. THE WOOD WAS SELECTED FOR THE VARI-
OUS PARTS OF THE GUITARS. NECKS, BACKS, TOPS AND SIDES
WERE BEING CUT AND SANDED. BODY SIDES WERE BEING ROUTED
OUT FOR THE WHITE BINDING. THAT'S WHEN I FIRST SAW "RED" .
HE WAS ROUTING AWAY, WOOD DUST FLYING EVERY WHERE, HE
STOPPED, LIFTED HIS PROTECTION MASK AND GAVE ME HIS SPE-
CIAL "SO WHO THE HELL ARE YOU" ? LOOK. WE LAUGHED ABOUT
THAT FOR YEARS.

ONE TIME HENRY THE FREIGHT ELEVATOR OPERATOR ASKED
ME TO COME DOWN TO THE SECOND FLOOR BECAUSE SOMEONE
WANTED TO SEE ME. I ASKED HIM WHO IT WAS. HE TOLD ME IT WAS
THE "SHYLOCK." THE DICTIONARY DISCRIPTION OF THIS WORD IS "A

RUTHLESS AND DEMANDING MONEY LENDER" . WOW!!! NO ITS NOT THAT BAD. HE ASKED ME FOR THE MONEY I OWED HIM. I TOLD HIM I DIDN'T OWE HIM ANYTHING AND I'D GET BACK TO HIM. A LOT OF THE WORKERS, INCLUDING THE FOREMAN AND OFFICE PERSON-NEL PLAYED THE NUMBERS AND HORSES AND ALWAYS OWED THIS GUY MONEY. THEY ALSO USED OTHER PEOPLES NAMES IF THEY OWED TOO MUCH MONEY AND COULDN'T GET ANY MORE CREDIT. I WAS NOT A GAMBLER. HENRY TOLD ME THAT RED USED MY NAME BECAUSE HE KNEW THIS GUY DIDN'T KNOW ME. I PAID REDS TAB AND WE LAUGHED ABOUT IT ALL THE TIME.

FROM THE WOOD SHOP WE WENT TO THE FINISHING ROOM AND MET JOHNNY DEROSA THE FOREMAN. I FORGOT TO MENTION THE FOREMAN'S NAME IN THE WOODSHOP, JERRY PERITO. HIS COUSIN VINNY WHO WAS THERE LONGER THAN ANYONE, USED TO BE IN CHARGE. HE NOW WORKED ON SPECIAL ORDERS. HE WORKED THERE BEFORE FRED GRETSCH JR. BILL GRETSCH WAS IN CHARGE WHEN HE STARTED THERE AS A TEENAGER.HE ALWAYS SAID BILL GRETSCH WAS THE GREATEST. FRED TOOK OVER AFTER HIS BROTHER DIED. VINNY FELT BETRAYED WHEN FRED SOLD THE COMPANY TO BALDWIN PIANO CO.

THE COLORS OF THE GUITARS ALL HANGING IN THE FINISH-ING ROOM WAS EYE CATCHING BUT THE SMELL OF THE LACQUER WASN'T. I HAD TO GET OUT OF THERE FAST. JIMMY WEBSTER WAS RESPONSIBLE FOR THESE MAGNIFICENT COLORS. JUST ONE OF MANY GOOD IDEAS JIMMY HAD FOR THE GRETSCH GUITAR. THE FOREMAN JOHN DEROSA ALSO STARTED THERE VERY YOUNG. HE WAS A VERY QUIET LAID BACK KIND OF GUY WHO WORKED HIS

BUTT OFF. HIS HANDS WERE SCARRED. THEY LOOKED LIKE SOME-ONES FEET WHO NEVER WORE SHOES. I COULDN'T BELIEVE IT. I USED TO ASK HIM TO "FEET" ME THE GUITAR, HE WOULD LAUGH LIKE CRAZY. JOHN DIDN'T LAUGH TOO OFTEN HE WAS VERY SERI-OUS AND VERY CONSCIENTIOUS ABOUT HIS JOB. ALL THE YEARS OF HAVING HIS HANDS SUBJECTED TO SAND PAPER AND PAINT THINNERS HAD TAKEN ITS TOLL ON HIS HANDS. HE WAS ALSO UPSET WHEN FRED SOLD THE COMPANY.WHEN JOHN PAINTED A GUITAR BY HIMSELF DOING ALL THE DIFFERENT OPERATIONS IT WAS A THING OF BEAUTY.

I REMEMBER ONE TIME IN THE PAINT SHOP SOMEONE PUT THEIR LUNCH ON ONE OF THE HEATING PIPES AND FORGOT ABOUT IT. IT STARTED TO SMOKE A LOT SETTING OFF THE SPRINKLERS. THERE WAS WATER EVERYWHERE. WORKERS WERE RUNNING AROUND ALL SOAKED. THE FIRE DEPARTMENT CAME ALSO. WHEN EVERYTHING SETTLED DOWN I WALKED OVER TO JOHN WHO BY THEN LOOKED LIKE "SWAMP THING" AND SAID TO HIM "I TOLD YOU NOT TO SMOKE" HE DIDN'T LAUGH.

BEFORE MY FIRST VISIT TO THE ASSEMBLY DEPARTMENT I WANT TO TELL YOU ABOUT MY FIRST GUITAR. YOU WILL NOT BE-LIEVE THIS. I STARTED TEACHING MYSELF TO PLAY WHEN I WAS ABOUT TWELVE YEARS OLD. MY FATHER PLAYED THE GUITAR AND SANG. THAT OLD GIBSON ACCOUSTIC GUITAR HELPED FEED MY MOTHER, BROTHER AND MYSELF DURING THE DEPRESSION, CIRCA 1929- 1940. HE HAD THESE MUSIC SHEETS WITH THE GUITAR CHORD BOXES ON THEM, HE SHOWED ME WHAT TO DO. HE WAS MY FIRST GUITAR HERO. I USED THIS GUITAR UNTIL I WAS TWENTY

THREE YEARS OLD. I WENT IN THE MARINE CORPS. AT AGE TWEN-
TY AND GOT OUT WHEN I WAS TWENTY TWO. I COULDN'T WAIT TO
GET BACK TO PLAYING THE GUITAR. ONE NIGHT WHILE I WAS IN
THE MARINES I WAS IN A BAR WITH SOME OF MY BUDDIES IN JACK-
SONVILLE NORTH CAROLINA. THERE WAS A GUITAR AND PIANO
DUO PLAYING. AFTER HAVING A FEW BEERS I BET THE GUYS THAT
I COULD GET UP THERE AND PLAY THE GUITAR. I WENT UP AND
ASKED THE GUITAR PLAYER IF I COULD PLAY AND HE SAID YES. I
PLAYED "THE WORLD IS WAITING FOR THE SUNRISE "AND" WHIS-
PERING". I HAD FREE BEERS THE REST OF THE NIGHT. ANYWAY,
WHEN I GOT OUT I STARTED PRACTICING. ONE NIGHT MY FRIENDS
AND I WENT TO SEE A GUY PLAY. I DON'T REMEMBER HIS NAME BUT
HE WAS A GOOD PLAYER, ABOUT TWENTY YEARS OLDER THAN
ME. HE HAD A D'ANGELICO GUITAR. MY FRIEND KNEW HIM SO WE
STARTED TO TALK. HE TOLD ME HE HAD A NEW TYPE OF GIBSON
GUITAR THAT HE COULD'T GET USED TO PLAYING AS IT WAS VERY
DIFFERENT. WE WENT DOWN THE BASEMENT OF THE CLUB AND HE
OPENED THIS SLIMLINE BROWN GIBSON CASE. AT FIRST I DIDN'T
KNOW WHAT TO MAKE OF THIS SOLID BODY GIBSON "GOLD TOP
LES PAUL" GUITAR. YOU HAVE TO REMEMBER THIS WAS 1955 AND I
NEVER SAW A SOLID BODY GUITAR BEFORE.

CAN YOU BELIEVE IT? THE MOST SORT AFTER GUITAR IN THE
WORLD TODAY AND HERE IT WAS LOOKING UP AT ME. IT HAD TO
BE ONE OF THE FIRST ONES EVER MADE. I PICKED IT UP AND I
KNEW INSTANTLY THAT I WAS HOLDING THE FUTURE. I PLAYED
THIS GUITAR PROFESSIONALLY FOR ABOUT TEN YEARS, AND THEN
AFTER TRYING ALL THE GRETSCH GUITARS I SWITCHED TO A 6192

Dan Duffy

"GRETSCH COUNTRY CLUB GUITAR". IN THE FIFTIES AND SIXTIES A LOT OF THE STUDIO PLAYERS USED THIS MODEL GUITAR. IT WAS GOOD FOR ALL TYPES OF MUSIC.

GETTING BACK TO MY INTERVIEW WITH JIMMY WEBSTER FOR THE JOB, EVERYTHING WENT WELL. HE EXPLAINED EVERYTHING TO ME ABOUT THE NEW INSPECTION SYSTEM HE WANTED. GREEN "OK" CARD SIGNED BY ME AND HUNG ON THE GUITAR WHEN IT PASSED MY INSPECTION AND A "RED" CARD IF I REJECTED IT. EVERYONE WHO BOUGHT A GRETSCH GUITAR GOT A GREEN CARD HANGING ON IT. ONE TIME THE OWNER OF A STORE CALLED UP AND SAID HE RECEIVED A GUITAR WITHOUT THE "OK" CARD HANGING ON IT. THE OFFICE SAID THEY WOULD SEND HIM A CARD BUT HE INSISTED ON SENDING THE GUITAR BACK AND TO MAKE SURE THAT I INSPECTED IT. HE TOLD THEM THAT SINCE THE GRETSCH COMPANY PUT THIS INSPECTION SYSTEM IN HE HAD LESS PROBLEMS WITH THE GUITARS. WHEN I HEARD THIS I THOUGHT NOW IS THE TIME TO ASK FOR A RAISE. JIMMY TOLD ME DURING MY INTERVIEW THAT I'D HAVE A JOB FOR LIFE BUT I'D NEVER GET RICH. WELL HE WAS ONLY HALF RIGHT. I NEVER GOT RICH.

HERE IS THE STORY I CALL THE "THE POWER OF THE RED CARD". ONE DAY HAROLD WOODS CALLED ME DOWN TO THE FACTORY OFFICE TO PUT AN EMPTY CUP I LEFT THERE ON TOP OF A FILE CABINET IN THE WASTE PAPER BASKET. WE JUST HAD OUR MORNING MEETING AND WE ALL HAD OUR USUAL CUP OF COFFEE. I FORGOT AND LEFT MY CONTAINER THERE. HE WAS VERY NASTY AND SAID HE AND THE OFFICE GIRLS DIDN'T CLEAN UP AFTER ANYONE. LATER I CAME TO THE CONCLUSION THAT HE DIDN'T LIKE THE

INSPECTION THING THAT I WAS DOING. HE WAS THE FACTORY MAN-
AGER AND AN ENGINEER AND WAS RESPONSIBLE FOR THE PRO-
DUCTION AND QUALITY. THIS WAS NOT THE FIRST TIME HE SAID
SOMETHING ABOUT SOME TRIVIAL MATTER. ONE DAY A LOT OF
CHET ATKINS 6120 GUITARS CAME THRU WITH THE TAILPIECES ON
CROOKED. AS A RULE I WOULD JUST PUT A SMALL PIECE OF MASK-
ING TAPE ON THE GUITARS TAILPIECE AND THEY WOULD TAKE CARE
OF THE PROBLEM. THIS TIME I FILLED OUT THE RED CARDS AND
HUNG THEM ON THE GUITARS. I LISTED EVERY THING THAT WAS
WRONG, CROOKED TAILPIECE, FRETS BUZZING, CHECK BRIDGE,
BRIDGE IN WRONG PLACE, LOOSE ROD IN NECK, ADJUST NECK,
ETC; WHEN JIMMY WEBSTER TOOK HIS DAILY WALK TO SEE ME, HE
SAW ALL THE RED CARDS AND STARTED LOOKING AT THE GUITARS.
HE SAID I WAS DOING A GOOD JOB AND WENT BACK DOWN STAIRS.
I HEARD HE WENT INTO THE FACTORY OFFICE TO SEE WOODS AND
HAD ONE OF THEIR FAMOUS CONFRONTATIONS ABOUT THE QUAL-
ITY. THE FOLLOWING WEEK HAROLD WOODS CALLED ME IN HIS
OFFICE. HE SAID I WAS DOING A GOOD JOB, GAVE ME A RAISE AND
SPOKE TO ME IN A CIVIL MANNER EVER SINCE. ITS GOOD TO WAVE
THE RED FLAG ONCE IN AWHILE TO EXCITE THE BULL, BUT NEVER
THE WHITE ONE.

FINALLY BILL HAGNER WHO ALSO STARTED THERE YOUNG.
TOOK ME TO THE ASSEMBLY DEPARTMENT WHERE I FINALLY GOT
TO SEE THE FINISHED GUITARS. AT THAT TIME THE ASSEMBLERS
WERE SET UP IN STATIONS. THE FIRST PERSON CLEANED THE FIN-
GER BOARD AND PUT ON THE TUNING MACHINES. THE NEXT PER-
SON INSTALLED THE PICKUPS. THEN THE TAILPIECES AND STRINGS

WERE PUT ON. THE GUITAR WAS THEN PUT IN THE RACK AT THE TUNE AND ADJUST STATION. THIS PERSON WAS USUALLY A GUITAR PLAYER. HE WOULD LEVEL THE FRETS AND ROUND THEM OFF WITH VARIOUS SIZE FILES, SET THE ACTION AND BRIDGE AND THEN TEST IT TO SEE IF THERE WERE ANY BUZZES. THERE WERE ALWAYS GUITAR PLAYERS IN THE ASSEMBLY DEPARTMENT. I ASSUMED I WAS FINALLY GOING TO PLAY SOME OF THESE GUITARS. BILL INTRODUCED ME TO THE FOREMAN, I FORGET HIS NAME. THE FORMAN OF THE ASSEMBLY CHANGED OFTEN IN THOSE YEARS. LATER ON WHEN "RED" WAS MADE FOREMAN THE WHOLE ASSEMBLY DEPARTMENT TOOK A STEP FORWARD IN QUALITY.

BILL TOOK ME JUST OUT SIDE THE ASSEMBLY DEPARTMENT WHERE THERE WAS A DESK, A PHONE, A BENCH FOR POLISHING THE GUITARS AND A RACK OF EMPTY GUITAR CASES. HE SAID THIS WILL BE MY HOME BASE. THERE WAS A RACK OF ABOUT SIX GUITARS READY TO GO OUT TO CUSTOMERS. HE SAID SIT DOWN AND TRY THEM. AT LAST I WAS GOING TO PLAY. I PICKED UP THE GUITAR AND PLUGGED IN THE CHORD TO THE AMPLIFIER. THE GUITAR DIDN'T WORK. THE PICKUP WAS DEAD. I REACHED DOWN FOR THE JACK INPUT AND IT WAS LOOSE. I GAVE IT A TWIST AND IT CAME ON.

BILL LOOKED AT ME AND SAID THAT'S WHY I NEED YOU. IT WAS A STROKE OF LUCK. I FELT GOOD. I STARTED TO PLAY VARIOUS CHORDS AND SCALES GRADUALLY PICKING UP SPEED. I PLAYED FOR ABOUT FIVE MINUTES ENDING WITH THE CHROMATIC SCALE TO TEST EVERY FRET. THE GUITAR PLAYERS FROM THE ASSEMBLY DEPARTMENT CAME OUT AND NODDED THEIR APPROVAL. BILL

ALSO NODDED APPROVAL. I FELT BETTER THAN GOOD, WHAT EVER THAT IS.

BILL HAGNER STARTED THERE WHEN HE WAS A TEENAGER. HE WORKED THERE PART TIME AS AN OFFICE BOY. HE WENT FROM OFFICE BOY TO PRESIDENT. HE ALWAYS WORKED VERY HARD. WHEN THE COMPANY WAS SOLD HIS FACE SHOWED THE SIGNS OF A GREAT LOSS. HE WAS BETRAYED BUT NEVER SAID IT. AFTER AWHILE HE SEEMED TO ACCEPT IT AND MOVE ON. BUT WHEN HE WAS TOLD THE COMPANY WAS BEING MOVED TO ARKANSAS THINGS CHANGED. EVERY ONE WAS IN A STATE OF CONFUSION AND DISBELIEF. CAN THIS BE TRUE? DID FRED SELL US OUT? YES HE DID. AT FIRST I COULDN'T BELIEVE IT. TO ME FRED GRETSCH WAS ONE OF THE NICEST PEOPLE I EVER WORKED FOR. DURING THE GUITAR BOOM EVERYONE WORKED THEIR BUTTS OFF FOR HIM, WE PRODUCED SEVENTY GUITARS A DAY WHEN NEEDED. TWICE THE FOREMAN AND I EACH GOT A BONUS OF SEVENTY FIVE DOL-LARS. VERY FRUGAL I THOUGHT AFTER THE HUGE PROFITS THEY MADE. I TRULY BELIEVE THAT THESE HIGH PRODUCTION FIGURES PROMPTED THE SALE OF THE COMPANY. WE LITERALLY WORKED SO HARD WE ALL LOST OUR JOBS. TO TOP THINGS OFF WE WERE TOLD THAT IF WE LEFT THE COMPANY BEFORE THE FINAL OFFI-CAL CLOSING DAY WE WOULD NOT GET ANY SEVERANCE PAY. CAN YOU BELIEVE IT? NOW THEY WERE THREATENING US. "STAY AND LOAD THOSE TRUCKS WITH YOUR LIFES WORK AND LIKE IT!" THIS MAY SEEM A BIT HARSH BUT HOW ELSE CAN YOU TAKE IT. TO TOP THINGS OFF FOR ME, THE LAST DAY WAS UNBELIEVABLE. WHEN WE WERE HANDED OUR FINAL CHECKS I DIDN'T GET ANY SEVERANCE

Dan Duffy

PAY. AGAIN I'M STUNNED. IS ALL THIS REAL? AM I HEARING RIGHT? BILL SAID BECAUSE HALF OF MY SALARY WAS PAID BY THE OFFICE HE DIDN'T HAVE TO GIVE ME ANYTHING. I STORMED INTO FREDS OFFICE. I MUST HAVE LOOKED LIKE AN UNCAGED LION. I TOLD HIM WHAT HAPPENED AND HE IMMEDIATELY SAID TO COME IN THE FOLLOWING WEEK AND I COULD PICK UP MY CHECKS. I CALMED DOWN AND LEFT. THE FOLLOWING WEEK I WENT INTO FREDS OFFICE. ON MY WAY TO HIS OFFICE I PASSED THE GIRLS DILIGENTLY WORKING AS USUAL BUT THEIR SMILES WERE NOT THERE. IN TWO YEARS THEIR JOBS WOULD BE GONE. I WENT INTO FREDS OFFICE AND GOT MY CHECKS, FRED WISHED ME LUCK AND I THANKED HIM. ONCE AGAIN I PASSED THE GIRLS. THIS TIME THEY HALF SMILED, I NODDED BACK. I WENT OUT TO THE ELEVATOR, GOT ON, WENT DOWN TO THE LOBBY, OUT THE DOOR, AND I WAS GONE.

WELL THAT WAS THE WAY IT ENDED. LETS GET BACK ONCE AGAIN TO THE BEGINNING AND MY FIRST TOUR OF THE FACTORY. AFTER PLAYING THE GUITAR AT MY DESIGNATED TESTING AREA, BILL SHOWED ME MY NEXT RESPONSIBILTY, THE REPAIR DEPARTMENT. I WAS INTRODUCED TO A VERY HUMBLE MAN CARMINE COPPOLLA. HIS JOB WAS TO FIX ALL THE GUITARS THAT WERE RETURNED. HE TURNED OUT TO BE THE BEST GUITAR MECHANIC I WOULD EVER KNOW. ONCE WE GOT BACK A 6022 "RANCHER" ACOUSTIC GUITAR. THE BACK OF THE GUITAR WAS SMASHED. WHEN THE GUY FIRST CALLED ABOUT THE GUITAR HE SAID HIS WIFE HIT HIM WITH IT. HE SAID HE LOVED THIS GUITAR MORE THAN HIS WIFE AND SHE KNEW IT. HE BEGGED ME TO SEE IF I COULD SAVE HIS FIRST LOVE, HIS GRETSCH GUITAR. CARMINE REPAIRED

THE GUITAR TO ITS ORIGINAL CONDITION. THE GUY WAS SO HAPPY HE SENT ME A LETTER THANKING ME. HE ALSO SAID HE WAS NOW GETTING ALONG BETTER WITH HIS WIFE. I SHOWED THE LETTER TO CARMINE AND SAID "YOU NOT ONLY FIXED THE GUITAR, YOU SAVED THE MARRIAGE"

CARMINE SHOOK HIS HEAD AND WALKED AWAY SMILING.

I HAD MANY INSTANCES LIKE THIS. ANOTHER TIME A GUY'S GIRLFRIEND HIT HIM WITH HIS GRETSCH BLACK DUO JET AND BROKE HIS ARM. THE GUITAR FELL TO THE FLOOR AND BROKE THE NECK. HE CALLED ME AND WAS CRYING ON THE PHONE "PLEASE HELP ME" I ASSURED HIM THAT WE WOULD. ANOTHER FAMOUS RHYTHM GUITAR PLAYER CAME TO THE FACTORY TO SEE ME. HE HAD THIS BIG 6040 GRETSCH ACOUSTIC GUITAR. THE HEADPIECE WAS SNAPPED OFF.

HE TOLD ME THAT HE ALWAYS TOOK HIS GUITAR TO BED WITH HIM TO PLAY HIMSELF TO SLEEP. DURING THE NIGHT HE ROLLED OVER ON IT AND BROKE THE NECK. THIS ACTUALLY HAPPENED TWICE.

MOST PEOPLE DON'T UNDERSTAND A PLAYERS ATTACHMENT TO HIS GUITAR. I NEVER LIKED ANYONE TOUCHING MY GUITAR. I ALWAYS LIVED BY THIS CODE. DON'T TOUCH MY GUITAR, DON'T TOUCH MY AMP, AND DON'T TOUCH MY WIFE. IN THAT ORDER.

THE REPAIR DEPARTMENT WOULD BECOME MY TEACHER. WHAT BETTER WAY COULD I FIND OUT WHAT GOES WRONG WITH THE GUITARS ONCE THEY LEAVE THE FACTORY. AT FIRST GLANCE IT LOOKED LIKE MORE GUITARS CAME BACK EVERY DAY THAN WERE SHIPPED OUT. NO WONDER THEY HIRED ME. I FIGURED THEY

NEEDED SOMEONE TO FIX THE SITUATION OR SOMEONE TO BLAME
IT ON. ON THE LATTER I WAS WRONG. EVERYONE CO-OPERATED
WITH ME FROM THE BEGINNING. THE RETURNS WOULD BE A TOUGH
PROBLEM. THE FIRST THING I WANTED TO DO WAS MAKE SURE
EVERY GUITAR PLAYED. A PLAYER WILL ACCEPT CERTAIN FINISH
FLAWS IF THE GUITAR PLAYS GOOD. I SHOWED A FINGERBOARD
TO THE FOREMAN IN THE ASSEMBLY DEPARTMENT, ONE THAT CAR-
MINE DID. THE FRETS WERE SMOOTH AND POLISHED. I ASKED HIM
TO PLAY THE GUITAR AFTER ABOUT ONLY TEN SECONDS HE SAID
IT PLAYED LIKE A DREAM. HE AGREED THAT THIS IS THE WAY THE
GUITARS SHOULD PLAY. WHEN A GUITAR FEELS GOOD AND PLAYS
GOOD THERE IS NOTHING BETTER. EVEN A NEW SET OF STRINGS
CAN GIVE A GUITAR NEW LIFE. ONE DAY A PLAYER BROUGHT HIS
GUITAR INTO THE FACTORY COMPLAINING ABOUT EVERY THING.
HE SAID THE GUITAR WAS ONLY A YEAR OLD AND NOW IT WOULDN'T
STAY IN TUNE AND HE WAS SORRY HE BOUGHT IT. I ASSURED
HIM EVERY THING WOULD BE FINE BUT IT WOULD TAKE ABOUT
AN HOUR. I GAVE THE GUITAR TO CARMINE. HE LOOKED AT THE
NECK AND SAID HE DIDN'T SEE ANYTHING WRONG.I SAID I KNOW,
JUST CHANGE THE STRINGS. AFTER AWHILE I BROUGHT THE GUI-
TAR BACK TO HIM. HE TRIED THE GUITAR AND STARTED TO RAVE
HOW GREAT THE GUITAR WAS. HE ASKED ME WHAT I DID AND I
HANDED HIM A SET OF STRINGS AND A POLISHING CLOTH. I TOLD
HIM TO CHANGE THE STRINGS MORE OFTEN AND ALWAYS WIPE
THE STRINGS OFF WHEN HE'S FINISHED PLAYING. HE WENT AWAY
HAPPY. LIKE I SAID, NEW STRINGS START THE HONEYMOON ALL
OVER AGAIN.

THE MAIN PROBLEM WITH ALL THE RETURNS WAS THE NECKS COMING LOOSE FROM THE BODY. WHAT A DISASTER. I IMMEDIATELY PICTURED MYSELF CHECKING IN THE RETURNS LIKE I DID EVERY DAY AND SEEING A GUITAR, BRAND NEW, WITH THE "OK" CARD HANGING ON IT AND SIGNED BY ME. WELL THE NIGHTMARE CAME TRUE. I WAS ON "ELM" STREET AND "FREDDIE KRUGER" WAS CHASING ME. IN ONE OF HIS HANDS, WITH THOSE LONG DAGGER LIKE FINGERNAILS, HE HELD A GUITAR BODY AND IN THE OTHER HAND A GUITAR NECK AND SWINGING IT AT ME. I COULD HEAR HIM SCREAMING "WAKE UP MAN AND DO YOUR JOB". GETTING BACK TO REALITY, I ASKED CARMINE WHAT HE THOUGHT WAS CAUSING THIS PROBLEM. HE WAS RELUCTANT TO SAY, NOT WANTING TO CAUSE PROBLEMS FOR ANYONE. I EXPLAINED TO HIM THAT THE PRESENT SITUATION WAS VERY BAD FOR THE IMAGE OF THE COMPANY. IT WAS SIMPLE I SAID. A BAD IMAGE MEANS LESS SALES, LESS SALES EQUALS NO MONEY, NO MONEY, NO BUSINESS, NO JOB.

I LOOKED AT A GUITAR THAT CAME BACK. I COULD SEE THAT THE DOVETAIL FIT WAS VERY LOOSE. CARMINE SAID THAT A GOOD DOVETAIL FIT DOESN'T EVEN HAVE TO BE GLUED. WELL, THAT MIGHT BE STRETCHING IT A BIT I THOUGHT. I LOOKED AT ANOTHER ONE AND IT HAD SHIMS IN IT. WHEN THE NECK IS FITTED TO THE BODY A CERTAIN NECK PITCH OR ANGLE IS NEEDED. WHEN THE WORKER CHISELED OUT THE DOVETAIL FIT TO SET THE PROPER NECK PITCH HE TOOK OUT TOO MUCH WOOD. WOOD SHIMS DO NOT HOLD UP UNDER THE TENSION OF THE STRINGS. WELL I THINK EVERY ONE IN THE FACTORY KNEW THIS BECAUSE WHEN I SHOWED THEM THEY ACTED AS IF THEY KNEW.

A GOOD STANDARD NECK PITCH MUST BE ESTABLISHED. ALL THE GUITARS MUST BE THE SAME. THE HEIGHT OF THE STRINGS DEPENDS ON THE NECK PITCH. IF THE NECK PITCH IS OFF, THE BASE OF THE BRIDGES HAVE TO BE BUILT UP OR CUT DOWN. THEY LOOK WRONG, THEY ARE WRONG, AND THEIR UGLY.IF ITS AN ELECTRIC GUITAR AND THE NECK IS PITCHED BACK OR FORWARD TOO MUCH THE STRINGS WILL HIT THE PICK UPS. BESIDES CUTTING DOWN THE BRIDGE BASE YOU HAVE TO CUT THE TOP BRACES TO LOWER THE PICKUP.

ONE DAY HAROLD WOODS CALLED ME DOWN TO THE FACTORY OFFICE. HE TOLD ME WE WERE GOING TO THE NEW YORK TESTING LABORATORY WITH TWO GUITARS. THEY DID EVERY THING TO THEM SHORT OF USING A HAND GRENADE TO SEPARATE THE NECK FROM THE BODY. WHEN WE GOT BACK AND HAROLD WOODS WAS TALKING ABOUT THE RESULTS TO JIMMY WEBSTER. JIMMY SAID THAT ONLY PROVES WE CAN DO IT. WE ALREADY KNOW WE CAN DO IT BECAUSE WE DID IT FOR YEARS. JIMMY SAID THE ONLY SOLUTION WAS A LARGE SCREW. HE ASKED ME WHAT I THOUGHT AND I SAID I DON'T KNOW. I WASN'T REALLY IN FAVOR OF GOING AGAINST THE TRADITIONAL CONSTRUCTION.

WE HAD A PROBLEM AND IT HAD TO BE SOLVED. SAMPLES WERE MADE AND TESTED. THE SCREW WAS COVERED BY A BLACK ROUND INSERT AND LOOKED GOOD. IT GOT THE NAME "NECK LOCK"

LETS STOP THIS SERIOUS THINKING FOR A MINUTE. TALKING ABOUT THESE SOLID BODY GUITARS REMINDS OF THE STORY I CALL "I HAD TO GO TO COURT BECAUSE I PLAYED A SOLID BODY

GUITAR".

FRED GRETSCH CALLED ME TO HIS OFFICE AND SAID HE HAD A PROBLEM AND WOULD I HELP HIM WITH IT. I SAID OF COURSE. HE SAID THE FOREIGN GUITAR MAKERS WERE SENDING THEIR AL- READY INEXPENSIVE INSTRUMENTS INTO THE UNITED STATES"DUTY FREE." THEIR CLAIM IS "ITS NOT A COMPLETE INSTRUMENT WITH- OUT THE AMPLIFIER." HE ASKED ME IF I COULD PLAY THE GUITAR WITHOUT THE AMP AND I SAID YOU CAN'T PLAY A "GIG" BECAUSE THEY CAN'T HEAR YOU BUT YOU CAN PRACTICE AT HOME WITHOUT THE AMP. HE ASKED ME "WHAT'S A GIG." FRED WAS NOT VERY HIP SO I EXPLAINED THAT A MUSICIAN CALLS A JOB A "GIG" I WENT ON TO SAY, I EVEN CALLED WORKING FOR HIM MY "GRETSCH GIG." HE SMILED AND SAID "PEOPLE HAVE CALLED WORKING FOR HIM MANY THINGS BUT NEVER A GIG." HE SAID "I LIKE THAT."

HE REALLY LOOKED AMAZED WHEN I TOLD HIM THAT I SPENT ABOUT SEVEN YEARS IN THE BATHROOM PRACTICING WITH MY SOLID BODY GUITAR. IT WAS A VERY LARGE ROOM. I HAD PLENTY OF ROOM FOR MY CHAIR, BOOKS, MUSIC STAND AND GUITAR. IT WAS VERY QUIET AND PRIVATE MOST OF THE TIME. THE ACOUS- TICS WERE GREAT.

FRED LOOKED AT ME WITH GREAT INTEREST. YOU COULD SEE HE WAS THINKING VERY DEEPLY ALMOST CUNNING. HE THEN ASKED ME IF A SOLID BODY GUITAR COULD BE HEARD IN A COURT ROOM WITHOUT THE AMP. I HESITATED A MOMENT THINKING HOW QUIET A COURT ROOM MUST BE AND SAID YES. HE THEN ASKED WOULD I GO TO WASHINGTON D.C. AND DEMONSTRATE THE GUI- TAR WITHOUT THE AMP. IN A COURT HEARING THE FOLLOWING

WEEK. STILL BEING "GUNG HO" I JUMPED AT THE CHANCE.

THE FLIGHT LEFT AT 9AM FROM LA GUARDIA AIRPORT. IT WAS ONLY AN HOUR FLIGHT. WHEN I GOT ON THE PLANE THE STEWARD-ESS SAID GOOD MORNING, CHECKED MY TICKET, DIRECTED ME TO MY SEAT AND SAID "YOU CAN PUT THAT THING IN THE OVER HEAD COMPARTMENT" I HATED WHEN PEOPLE CALLED MY GUITAR "A THING." "HEY DUFF GO HOME AND GET YOUR THING AND LETS HAVE SOME FUN" THAT'S WHAT I HEARD WHEN I WAS A KID. GOD, I HATED THAT.

"HERE'S MY THING" I GESTURED. THEN I'D GET MY GUITAR.

ALL THE WRINKLED "SUITS" HAD STARED AT ME WHEN I WALKED PAST THEM ON MY WAY TO MY SEAT. THESE GUYS ALL LOOKED LIKE LAWYERS. THEY LOOKED AT ME LIKE I WAS A "BEAT-NIK" WITH A SUIT ON. THEY KNEW I WASN'T ONE OF THEM BECAUSE MY SUIT WAS PRESSED. I COULD HEAR THEM THINKING WHO IS THIS GUY. THIS COULD BE THE GUY WHO'S GONNA PLAY THE GUI-TAR IN THE COURT ROOM. HIS SUIT IS PRESSED, WE'RE GONNA LOSE, LETS THROW HIM OFF THE PLANE. I DID THIS FOR THREE DAY'S. I WORE A DIFFERENT CLEAN PRESSED SUIT EVERY DAY.

THE WRINKLED SUITS WERE LOOKIING WORSE EVERY DAY. THEY KEPT CHECKING ME OUT. THEY WERE GETTING SCARED. I WAS GETTING MORE CONFIDENT.

WHEN I FINALLY WENT INTO THE COURT ROOM THE COURT CLERK ESCORTED ME TO MY SEAT. I WAS IN FRONT OF A PANEL OF SIX MEN. I DIDN'T RECOGNIZE ANY OF THEM FROM THE PLANE. I KNOW THEY WERE PART OF THE CLAN BECAUSE THEIR SUITS WERE WRINKLED. THEY SAT THERE LOOKING AT ME AND MY GUI-

TAR. THEIR GLASSES HUNG ON THE END OF THEIR NOSE AND EACH HAD A PENCIL IN HIS HAND. THEY STARTED TO LOOK LIKE MY NUNS IN CATHOLIC GRAMMER SCHOOL WHEN I WAS YOUNG, I STARTED TO SWEAT. THEY ASKED ME IF IT WAS TRUE THAT I PLAYED MY SOLID BODY GUITAR IN THE BATHROOM FOR SEVEN YEARS. I ANSWERED YES. THEN THEY ASKED ME TO PLAY. IMMEDIATELY I STARTED TO THINK "WHAT IF THE NECK COMES OFF WHILE I WAS PLAYING." I STARTED TO PLAY ANYWAY. I KNEW THEY COULD HEAR ME BECAUSE ONE OF THE SUITS STARTED TO TAP HIS PENCIL TO THE RHYTHM I WAS PLAYING AND HE WAS SMILING. HE WAS HAVING A GOOD TIME. I FORGAVE HIM FOR HIS SUIT. WHEN I FINISHED PLAYING THEY SAID "THANK YOU MISTER DUFFY" I SAID "MY PLEASURE" AND LEFT. A FEW MONTHS LATER FRED TOLD ME HE WON THE CASE BUT NOW THEY WERE SENDING IN THE GUITARS WITHOUT STRINGS TO BEAT THE DUTY TAX. I SAID "SORRY I CAN'T HELP YOU WITH THIS ONE."

GETTING BACK TO THE SCREW IN THE NECK, EVERYONE AGREED TO THE NEW "NECK LOCK SYSTEM." JIMMY SURE HAD A WAY WITH WORDS. HE COULD ALWAYS TURN A NEGATIVE INTO A POSITIVE. I'M SURE HE'S MAKING LIFE BETTER FOR EVERYONE WHERE EVER HE IS.

ONE DAY JIMMY CAME TO MY TESTING BOOTH WITH PICTURES OF NEW BMW CARS. HE WENT ON AND ON ABOUT THE ONE HE WAS GOING TO BUY. EVERY TIME HE WAS IN HE WOULD SHOW ME PICTURES OF A DIFFERENT MODEL. HE COULDN'T MAKE UP HIS MIND. FINALLY ONE DAY HE CAME IN AND TOLD ME HE BOUGHT A NEW CAR. A **DODGE.** I COULDN'T BELIEVE IT.

I SAID THERE'S A BIG DIFFERENCE BETWEEN A DODGE AND A BMW. HE SAID I KNOW "THE PRICE." HE THEN WENT ON TO TELL ME ALL ABOUT THE DODGE. WHAT A GREAT CAR IT WAS. AFTER A WHILE HE WAS HAVING TROUBLE WITH IT I DIDN'T SAY ANYTHING, THEN ONE DAY HE CAME AND TOLD ME THAT WE HAD TO GO TO NEW ENGLAND AND SEE A GUITAR PICKUP SOMEONE HAD. HE SAID WE WOULD GO IN HIS BMW. HE SAID THAT HE TRADED THE LEMON IN FOR A REAL CAR. WE LEFT EARLY ONE DAY AND WERE ON THE THRUWAY ROLLING ALONG AT A GOOD PACE. HE TURNED TO ME AND SAID "RUNS GOOD?" I SAID GREAT. HE HAD THAT STINKING PIPE HANGING CLINCHED BETWEEN HIS TEETH. HE HAD THAT LIT-TLE SMILE ON HIS FACE AS HE WAS SLYLY LOOKING OVER AT ME. WE WERE DOING A HUNDRED MILES PER HOUR. I PRETENDED I DIDN'T KNOW. SOON AFTER HE SLOWED DOWN, PULLED OVER AND STOPPED.

WE LOOKED AT EACH OTHER WITH NO EXPRESSION AT ALL, AND THEN WE BURST INTO TEARS OF LAUGHTER, WE COULDN'T STOP. EVENTUALLY HE SAID "DON'T TELL ANYONE" AND WE WERE ON OUR WAY AGAIN.

THE REPAIR DEPARTMENT WAS SUFFERING FROM A VERY BAD OLD DECISION TO GIVE A LIFETIME GUARANTEE ON THE NECK. GUITARS THAT WERE TWENTY TO THIRTY YEARS OLD WERE BEING SENT BACK FOR NECK REPLACEMENT OR REPAIR. I HAD TO HONOR THE GUARANTEE BUT I WOULD CHARGE TO REPLACE THE FRETS AS THEY WERE WORN DOWN TO THE FINGER BOARD. OTHER CHARGES WERE BEING IMPLEMENTED FOR OBVIOUS ABUSE OR NEGLECT. SOME OF THESE GUITARS WERE PROBABLY STORED IN

VERY DAMP PLACES FOR YEARS. EVER SO OFTEN WE WOULD GET ONE BACK AND WHEN I OPENED THE CASE A MUSTY AND PUNGENT ODOR LEAPED OUT AT ME. I WOULD GET A RAG AND HOLD THE GUITAR BY THE NECK AND PLACE IT HIGH IN THE RACK NEAR THE OPEN WINDOW AND THE CLOSED CASE NEXT TO IT. I FOUND A SPRAY AT THE LOCAL HARDWARE STORE TO HELP NEUTRALIZE THE ODOR. CARMINE TOLD ME THE ODOR CAME FROM THE ANIMAL GLUE USED AT THAT TIME TO SECURE THE PLUSH LINING OF THE CASE. IF THE GUITAR TOUCHED YOUR CLOTHING YOU SMELL LIKE YOU PASSED AWAY SIX MONTHS AGO AND YOU WEREN'T BURIED. WHEN THE REPAIR WAS FINISHED I WOULD NOTIFY THE CUSTOMER AND TELL THEM THEY NEEDED A NEW CASE. THEY USUALLY AGREED. ONCE A GUY TOLD ME THE SMELL DIDN'T BOTHER HIM AND DIDN'T UNDERSTAND WHY I WAS MAKING SUCH A BIG "STINK" ABOUT IT. I HAD TO PUT THIS NOW BEAUTIFUL GUITAR INTO A USED COFFIN.

SEEING AND PLAYING A TWENTY FIVE YEAR OLD "CATS EYE" GUITAR MADE MY JOB VERY INTERESTING. THIS WAS A COLLECTORS DREAM JOB. I OFTEN WONDERED ABOUT THE GUITAR AS I PLAYED IT. WHERE ITS BEEN, WHO PLAYED IT OR WAS IT BOUGHT AND PLAYED JUST ONCE AND FOR SOME REASON PUT IN THE ATTIC FOR TWENTY YEARS. I HAD SUCH A GUITAR IN MY HANDS ONE DAY. THE GUITAR WAS SO GOOD I CALLED THE GUY TO SEE IF HE WOULD SELL IT TO ME. HE TOLD ME HE COULDN'T BECAUSE IT WAS HIS FATHERS GUITAR WHO NEVER CAME BACK FROM OVERSEAS DURING WORLD WAR TWO. HE NEVER KNEW HIM AND THE GUITAR WAS ALL HE HAD OF HIS. HE CALLED ME THROUGH THE YEARS EVERY TIME HE BOUGHT A GUITAR FROM THE LOCAL MUSIC STORE. THE

STORE WOULD ORDER IT WITH SPECIAL INSTRUCTIONS FOR ME TO PICK IT OUT. BEFORE LONG ALL HIS FRIENDS WERE ORDERING GUITARS AND I HAD TO PICK THEM OUT. I NEVER CALLED ANYONE AGAIN ABOUT THEIR GUITAR. OLD GUITARS HAVE SPECIAL STORIES, I WISH THEY COULD TELL THEM. ALL EXCEPT MINE.

"BUY A GRETSCH GUITAR AND BLEED TO DEATH WHILE YOUR PLAYING IT" THIS IS THE BOLD PRINT I PICTURED ON THE COVERS OF ALL THE GUITAR MAGAZINES WHEN GUITARS WERE BEING RETURNED BECAUSE THE FRETS WERE STICKING OUT OF THE SIDES OF THE FINGERBOARD. THE EBONY FINGERBOARDS WERE SHRINKING AND ANOTHER NIGHTMARE BEGINS. NOW WHAT DO WE DO. WE WERE PAYING FOR PURE LONG TERM DRIED WOOD. IT WAS ALWAYS CHECKED FOR THE MOISTURE CONTENT WHEN WE RECEIVED IT. WE STACKED THE FINGERBOARDS FOR MONTHS. WE EVEN ROTATED THEM. THIS HAPPENED EVERY ONCE IN AWHILE. THIS PROBLEM WAS NEVER REALLY RESOLVED. LATER IN MY CAREER WHEN I WAS WORKING FOR AN IMPORTER OF BRAZILIAN ROSE WOOD GUITARS I SAW A CONTINUING DISASTER.THEY EVEN SENT ME TO THE FACTORY IN BRAZIL. MY CONCLUSION OF WHAT I CALL WET WOOD IS "YOU CAN THAW IT YOU CAN STORE IT, YOU CAN DYE IT YOU CAN FRY IT" AND IT WILL STILL WARP ON OCCASION. IT CAUSES MOST OF ALL THE PROBLEMS IN GUITAR CONSTRUCTION.

HERE IS A STORY I CALL "THE CASE OF THE SWINGING CLARINET" THIS DOES NOT MEAN SWINGING IN A MUSICAL SENSE, BUT A CLARINET SWINGING BY A ROPE FROM A SEVENTH FLOOR BALCONY OR WINDOW I'M NOT SURE WHICH. FOR THOSE NOT FAMILIAR WITH THE GRETSCH BUILDING AT SIXTY BROADWAY BROOKLYN IT IS A

BLOCK LONG, A BLOCK WIDE WITH A SMALL PARKING LOT IN THE REAR FOR SUITS ONLY, AND IT IS TEN STORIES HIGH WITH EACH LEVEL HAVING AN EXTREMELY HIGH CEILING, IN OTHER WORDS IT IS BIG. THE GRETSCH COMPANY OCCUPIED THE SEVENTH AND NINTH FLOORS. THIS GUY WAS SENDING DOWN INSTRUMENTS ON A ROPE TO THE PARKING LOT BELOW. HE WAS ON THE SEVENTH FLOOR. FRED ALSO HAD A MUSICAL ACCESSORY WHOLESALE BUSINESS THAT TOOK UP ONE HALF OF THE SEVENTH FLOOR. I GUESS THIS GUY WAS GOING TO SEND DOWN THE WHOLE BUSINESS PIECE BY PIECE ON THAT ROPE.IT'S A GOOD THING THAT SOMEONE SAW THAT CLARINET SWINGING IN THE BREEZE. THE WHOLE BUILDING IS NOW BEING CONSTRUCTED INTO VERY EXPENSIVE CONDOS. I'M SURE THE ECHOS OF ME PLAYING THE "FRED GRETSCH BLUES" (THE CHROMATIC SCALE I USED FOR TESTING) STILL HAUNTS THE BUILDING.

LETS GO BACK TO THE REPAIR DEPARTMENT AND TALK ABOUT FLAT TOP GUITARS. ALL THESE GUITARS LOOKED GOOD AND SOUNDED GOOD BUT CARMINES RACKS WOULD ALWAYS HAVE A FEW GUITARS TO REPAIR. SOME OF THESE WERE CUSTOMER RE-TURNS AND SOME WERE NEW THAT I REJECTED. THIS COST THE COMPANY EXTRA MONEY BUT IS WAS WORTH IT. AS THE YEARS WENT ON THE FLAT TOPS BECAME HIGHLY RESPECTED AND WE SOLD A LOT OF THEM.I MEAN A LOT!

MY FIRST GRIPE WAS WITH THE BIG BODY 6022 RANCHER GUITAR. THE TOP WOULD ALWAYS SINK DOWN AT THE SOUND HOLE IN FRONT OF THE BRIDGE AND AT THE END OF THE FINGERBOARD. WHEN I FIRST STARTED THERE THE TUNE AND ADJUST MECHAN-

IC WOULD INSTALL A RIDICULOUS LOOKING HIGH SADDLE IN THE BRIDGE. THIS I WOULD NOT ACCEPT. CARMINE SAID HE WOULD REPAIR THEM BUT IT WOULD TAKE TIME. MOST OF THE TIME THEY WERE MADE ACCEPTABLE. THOSE THAT WERE NOT GOT THE AX OR BECAME FIRE WOOD. AT FIRST I WASN'T TOO POPULAR WITH THE WOODSHOP BUT BILL HAGNER WOULD GET TOGETHER WITH CAR-MINE, VINNY, JERRY AND RED AND ALWAYS COME UP WITH A SOLU-TION.ADJUSTMENTS WERE MADE TO THE TOP AND THE BRACES. THE TOP WAS MADE WITH A SLIGHT CROWN TO IT WITH BRACES TO HOLD IT. ALL FLAT TOPS WOULD EVENTUALLY BE MADE THIS WAY. THE BRACING UNDER THE FINGERBOARD WAS CHANGED TO HELP HOLD IT UP IF OUR OLD FRIEND "WET WOOD "STARTED DRYING. AS A RULE NOTHING CAN HOLD BACK THE DRYING. IF IT DOES IT CRACKS AND HAS TO BE FIXED. THE RANCHER MODEL HAD A BIG DRIVING FORCE SOUND AND WAS A GOOD SELLER.

THE MODEL 6010 SUN VALLEY ACOUSTIC FLAT TOP WAS AN-OTHER GOOD SOUNDING GUITAR. IT WAS A GOOD LOOKER WHEN IT HAD ROSEWOOD BACK AND SIDES. ALL THE FLAT TOPS HAD SOLID SPRUCE TOPS. NOT MANY PROBLEMS WITH THIS GUITAR. IF YOU HAVE ONE OF THESE INSTRUMENTS CHERISH IT AND MAKE SURE YOUR SON OR GRANDSON DOES THE SAME.

THE FOLK GUITAR MODEL 6003 WAS ALWAYS A HUGE SELL-ER. THE LITTLE GUITAR WITH THE BIG SOUND. WE ALWAYS HAD BRIDGES COMING OFF THESE LITTLE MONSTERS. IF A BEGINNER STUDENT COULD AFFORD THIS GUITAR HE HAD AN ADVANTAGE. AN EASY PLAYING GUITAR IS VERY IMPORTANT, ESPECIALLY AT THE NUT. THE STRINGS HAD TO BE EASY TO PRESS DOWN AT THE NUT

BECAUSE THAT'S WHERE YOU BEGIN. GETTING THE STRINGS LOW WITH OUT HITTING THE FIRST FRET AND CAUSING A BUZZ WAS VERY TIME CONSUMING. THE "FRET NUT", WAS INTRODUCED AT THIS TIME. I DON'T KNOW WHERE THE NAME "ZERO FRET" CAME FROM. WITH THIS CHANGE ALL THE ACTIONS AT THE NUT WERE UNIFORM AND EASY TO PLAY

ONE OF THE BEST ACOUSTIC GUITARS MADE IN THE SIXTIES WAS THE NYLON CLASSICAL HAUSER MODEL. THIS GUITAR HAD A RICH FAT SOUND. IF YOU STARTED PLAYING ONE YOU COULDN'T PUT IT DOWN. I HAVE ONE. IT HAS CRACKS ALL OVER IT. I KEEP FIXING THEM WITH SMALL PIECES OF DIAMOND SHAPED SPRUCE WOOD. THE GUITAR IS A SIMPLE PIECE, MAHOGANY NECK, BACK, SIDES AND A SOLID SPRUCE TOP.

THE GUITAR WAS SENT TO FRED GRETSCH FOR HIS WHOLE-SALE MUSICAL INSTRUMENT BUSINESS. HE ASKED ME TO PLAY IT AND LET HIM KNOW WHAT I THOUGHT. THE GUITAR "SANG". I TOLD HIM IT WAS VERY GOOD AND WHY DON'T WE MAKE IT OURSELVES.

I TOLD HIM WE SHOULD MAKE THE GUITAR INSTEAD OF BUY-ING THEM, AND MAKE IT A PART OF THE GRETSCH LINE. WE DID JUST THAT.

AT FIRST WE HAD A LOT OF PROBLEMS WITH THE TOPS CRACKING. THAT'S RIGHT, OUR OLD FRIEND "WET WOOD" WAS VIS-ITING US AGAIN. WHEN IT STARTS DRYING IT CRACKS, ESPECIAL-LY DOWN THE CENTER OF THE TOP WHERE THE TWO PIECES OF SPRUCE WERE GLUED TOGETHER. CARMINE REPAIRED A LOT OF THESE. SOMETIMES IT WOULD CRACK AGAIN RIGHT ALONG SIDE THE PIECE OF SPRUCE THAT WAS USED TO FIX THE CRACK. SOME-

TIMES THE WOODSHOP WOULD MAKE THE TOP THICKER TO PRE-VENT THE CRACKING, THIS ONLY KILLED THE SOUND AND GOT ME TEED OFF. THINGS WORKED OUT BETTER WHEN THE TOPS WERE KEPT IN INVENTORY LONGER. MORE RAW MATERIAL EXPENSE WAS NECESSARY, BUT WORTH EVERY CENT. THIS WAS TRULY A TER-RIFIC GUITAR.

HERE'S A SHORT INTERESTING QUALITY CONTOL STORY. SHORTLY AFTER I WAS HIRED I WAS TESTING A CHET ATKINS GUI-TAR MODEL # 6120. AFTER TESTING IT FOR BUZZING FRETS BY PLAYING THE USUAL FRED GRETSCH BLUES I WOULD PLAY THE GUITAR FOR A WHILE. AS I WAS PLAYING MY USUAL REPERTOIRE OF SCALES, CHORDS AND TUNES I NOTICED THE GUITAR WAS NOT IN TUNE ABOVE THE 12 TH FRET. I BROUGHT THIS TO THE ATTEN-TION OF EVERYONE BUT NO ONE HAD THE ANSWER. SOME SAID I WAS HEARING THINGS. FINALLY VINNY CHECKED THE FRET SCALE AND SAID THE FRETS WERE OUT OF PLACE ABOVE THE 12TH FRET.

HE SAID THIS COULD HAVE HAPPENED WHEN THEY TOOK THE FRET SAW APART FOR SHARPENING AND WASN'T PUT BACK IN THE RIGHT POSITIONS. HAROLD WOODS DREW UP A NEW SCALE AND EVEN GAVE ME SOME RESPECT AFTER THAT. HE THREW MY EMPTY COFFEE CONTAINERS AWAY IF I FORGOT THEM.

ALL YOU CHET ATKINS FANS CHECK YOUR GUITARS. IF YOU HAVE ONE OF THESE GUITARS MADE AROUND 1956 OR 1957 SEND IT BACK TO THE FACTORY "WHERE EVER THAT IS" AND TELL THEM I SAID IT WAS "OK"

BACK IN THE REPAIR SHOP WE HAD AN OCCASIONAL RETURN OF AN ARCH TOP "F" HOLE ACOUSTIC GUITAR TO HAVE THE NECK

RESET. GRETSCH WAS REALLY RESPECTED FOR THESE GUITARS. THESE WERE USED MAINLY BY JAZZ AND COUNTRY PLAYERS.

THE "ELDORADO" BEING THE TOP OF THE LINE WAS A MAGNIFICENT LOOKING, PLAYING, AND SOUNDING GUITAR. NO I DON'T HAVE ONE BUT I WISH I DID. I'D PUT AN EMG JAZZ PICK UP ON IT AND PLAY IT TILL IT NEEDED A FRET JOB.

THE LINE OF ARCH TOPS WITH THE LAMINATED WOOD TOPS WERE ALSO GOOD SOUNDING INSTRUMENTS. THESE WERE CALLED "NEW YORKER" , "CORSAIR", "CONSTELLATION" AND I BELIEVE "SYNCHROMATIC".

SOMETIMES I WOULD MOUNT A PICKUP ON THE GUITAR, ONE OF THE DEARMAND PICKUPS THAT WE ALL USED ON OUR ACCOUSTIC GUITAR BACK THEN TO SEE WHAT KIND OF SOUND I WOULD GET FROM EACH DIFFERENT MODEL. ONCE I HAD A BEAUTIFUL ELDORADO MODEL MOUNTED UP FOR DAYS PLAYING IT. I PLAYED IT EVERY DAY UNTIL THE STORE CALLED AND WANTED TO KNOW "WHAT HAPPENED TO MY ORDER?"

EVER SO OFTEN A GUITAR WOULD HAVE THAT SOMETHING SPECIAL SOUND. THIS PROVES THAT EVERY THING CREATED EQUAL IS NOT EQUAL.

YES THE REPAIR DEPARTMENT AND CARMINE WERE MY TEACHER. HERE'S A "BELIEVE IT OR NOT STORY". ALL MY YEARS AT GRETSCH I NEVER FIXED A GUITAR WITH MY HANDS. I WASN'T HIRED TO DO THAT. I WAS ONLY TO TEST THE GUITAR AND TELL THEM WHAT I FOUND WRONG WITH IT. WHEN MY TOUR OF DUTY WAS OVER WITH GRETSCH I WENT BACK TO PLAYING AND TEACHING. AFTER ABOUT TWO YEARS A FRIEND CALLED ME AND TOLD

ME A COMPANY ON LONG ISLAND WAS LOOKING FOR ME. I CALLED
THEM AND THEY TOLD ME THEY WERE HAVING A LOT OF TROUBLE
WITH THEIR GUITARS AND WOULD I COME IN TO SEE THEM. THEY
IMPORTED GUITARS FROM JAPAN AND BRAZIL". AFTER A LONG IN-
TERVIEW I WAS HIRED. MOST OF THE INTERVIEW WAS ABOUT WHAT
I DID AT THE GRETSCH COMPANY AND THEY TOLD ME ABOUT THE
PROBLEMS THEY HAD.

WHEN I REPORTED FOR WORK THEY TOOK ME IN BACK TO
THE GUITAR DEPARTMENT. AT ONE GLANCE I COULD TELL THEY
SOLD A LOT OF GUITARS. EVERY DAY THE HEAD OF THE DEPART-
MENT WOULD RECEIVE A BUNCH OF ORDERS FROM THE FRONT
OFFICE. THE GUITARS WERE PULLED FROM INVENTORY AND GIVEN
TO THE SERVICE PEOPLE TO SERVICE BEFORE THEY WENT OUT.
THERE WAS ABOUT SIX OR SEVEN MEN DOING THIS WORK. THE
HEAD OF THE DEPARTMENT ASKED ME WHAT I WANTED TO DO
SO I SAID WHAT EVER YOU NEED. HE TOOK ME TO THE BACK AND
SHOWED ME ABOUT FIVE HUNDRED GUITARS FROM JAPAN THAT
HAD TAPE ON EACH ONE STATING WHAT WAS WRONG. I OPENED
ONE UP THAT SAID BAD NECK. ONE LOOK AND I KNEW THAT ALL IT
NEEDED WAS A NECK ADJUSTMENT WITH THE WRENCH. ANOTHER
SAID BAD PICKUP, PROBABLY THE JACK WIRE WAS OFF. I TOOK
THE TWO PIECES BACK TO THE DEPARTMENT WHERE HE GAVE ME
A BENCH AND SOME TOOLS. I FIXED THE TWO PIECES, AND GAVE
A SMALL CONCERT TO SHOW I COULD PLAY. I TOLD THE HEAD OF
THE DEPARTMENT TO BRING OUT SOME MORE OF THE PROBLEM
GUITARS. HE WAS ALL SMILES AND SAID SURE. WELL HE BROUGHT
OUT A SKID FULL. I FIXED ONE AFTER THE OTHER WITH ALL SORTS

OF PROBLEMS.

IT TOOK ME ABOUT TWO MONTHS TO FIX ALL THESE GUITARS. I WAS HAVING THE TIME OF MY LIFE. CARMINE WOULD BE PROUD OF ME. WELL (MAYBE) HE ALWAYS SAID "I FIX, YOU PLAY" I CAUGHT UP TO THE GUYS ON THE BENCH. I WAS FIXING THEM AS FAST AS THEY COULD REJECT THEM. A FEW OF THE GUYS QUIT. THE ONES WHO REMAINED DID A BETTER JOB. WHEN THEY HAD A PROBLEM I SHOWED THEM HOW TO FIX IT.

THE PRESIDENT (WHO WAS WATCHING ME EVERY DAY) TOLD ME THAT I WAS NOW IN CHARGE OF THE WHOLE GUITAR DEPART-MENT. HE GAVE ME A DESK AND A PHONE AND THEN HE HANDED ME A BONUS CHECK FOR ONE THOUSAND DOLLARS AND SAID THANK YOU. (BELIEVE IT OR NOT)

ONE OF THE GUITARS THAT YOU RARELY SEEN IN THE REPAIR DEPARTMENT WAS THE SOLID BODY MODEL 6134 "CORVETTE" THIS GUITAR HAS A UNIQUE DESIGN. ALL OTHER BOOKS ON GRETSCH GUITARS FAIL TO MENTION THE FACT THAT THE NECK HAS THE ADJUSTMENT ROD INSTALLED THE FULL LENGTH OF THE NECK. ALL OTHER MODELS ARE FROM THE HEAD PIECE TO THE TWELFTH FRET. THIS GUITAR WAS DESIGNED TO GIVE THE PLAYER TOTAL ACCESS TO ALL FRETS WITH NO EFFORT. THIS GUITAR WAS NO WAY COPIED FROM THE LESS PAUL JR. THESE NECKS ADJUSTED EASILY WHEN THERE WAS A PROBLEM. THEY WERE VERY RARELY RETURNED. THIS WAS MADE INTO VARIOUS MODEL GUITARS BY CHANGING THE COLORS AND PICKGUARD. THE TWIST AND PRIN-CESS MODELS TO NAME A FEW.

HEY, HEY, WE'RE THE "MONKEE'S" IS A SHORT STORY. WHEN

WE CREATED THIS MODEL GUITAR ACCORDING TO WHAT THEY WANTED, EVERY ONE THOUGHT THE "MONKEE" LOGO SHOULD APPEAR ON THE ROD SHIELD COVER AND THE PICK GUARD. AFTER WE STARTED SENDING THEM OUT, LITTLE BY LITTLE, REQUESTS CAME IN FOR REPLACEMENT ROD SHIELD COVERS AND PICKGUARDS WITHOUT THE (MONKEE) NAME ON THEM. THE REQUESTS BECAME SO GREAT THAT WE DECIDED TO SEND PLAIN PICKGUARDS AND ROD SHIELD COVERS INSIDE THE CASE WITH ALL NEW ORDERS. I GUESS NO ONE WANTED TO PLAY LIKE A MONKEE. COULD THEY PLAY? I DON'T KNOW.

THE MODEL 6199 JAZZ GUITAR ENDORSED BY SAL SALVADOR WAS A GOOD GUITAR. I BOUGHT ONE SHORTLY AFTER I WAS THERE AWHILE. IT HAD A GREAT SOUND BUT WAS PRONE TO FEED BACK. I HAD CARMINE INSTALL SOUND POSTS (WOODEN DOWELS) UNDER THE BRIDGE. THIS CUT SOME OF IT DOWN. THEN I GOT THE IDEA OF STUFFING IT. I USED FIBER GLASS, YOU KNOW THAT ITCHY STUFF. ON THE GIG THAT NIGHT I SHOOK MORE THAN "ELVIS" DID. SOMEHOW I GOT IT DOWN MY NECK AND WAS JUMPING OUT OF MY PANTS ALL NIGHT. THE NEXT DAY I EMPTIED THE FIBER GLASS FROM THE GUITAR INTO A BAG. I WAS ITCHY AGAIN. I HAD TO GET EVERY BIT OF IT OUT SO I BROUGHT IT TO WORK. I PUT THE AIR PRESSURE HOSE INSIDE THE GUITAR AND BLEW IT OUT. THE NEXT DAY SOME OF THE WORKERS COMPLAINED THEY HAD A TERRIBLE ITCH ALL NIGHT. I SAID "ME TOO"

I KNEW THIS WAS STUPID WHEN I WAS DOING IT. I DIDN'T SAY ANYTHING TO CARMINE ABOUT THIS, ESPECIALLY WHEN I SAW HIM SCRATCHING HIS BACK WITH A GUITAR NECK.

"SOMETHING EVIL THIS WAY COMES"

BACK IN THE REPAIR DEPARTMENT CARMINE WAS STANDING OVER THE BENCH WITH HIS HAMMER IN HAND ABOUT TO STRIKE THE BEAST THAT WAS LAYING THERE. WAS IT THE BEAST FROM TWENTY THOUSAND FATHOMS? NO? WAS IT "THE THING" FROM OUTER SPACE? NO, IT WAS THE GRETSCH "BIKINI" GUITAR AND BASS COMBO. CARMINE WAS ABOUT TO TRY TO SEPARATE THE GUITAR NECK FROM THE BODY. THE GUITAR SHAPED BODY WAS A SLAB OF WOOD CUT DOWN THE MIDDLE AND FOLDED IN HALF LIKE A BUTTERFLY. IT WAS HELD TOGETHER WITH SMALL HINGES. THERE WAS TRACKS MOUNTED WITH SCREWS. THE NECK WAS MOUNTED ON A PIECE OF WOOD AND SLIDES INTO THOSE RECEIV- ING TRACKS. THE NECK AND PIECE OF WOOD WAS THE COMPLETE GUITAR WITH TUNING MACHINES, STRINGS, PICK UP, TAIL PIECE ETC. THERE WAS A LOT OF PROBLEMS WITH THE ELECTRONICS BECAUSE ALL THE WIRING WAS JAMMED INTO A SMALL SPACE. THE BIG PROBLEM WAS THE TRACKS AND HINGES. THE PARTS WOULD NOT GO TOGETHER, AND WHEN THEY DID YOU COULDN'T GET THEM APART. THE SCREWS CAME OUT OF THE HINGES. THE BEAST ALWAYS FELL APART. IT WAS A PIECE OF CRAP. IT ALSO CAME IN A BASS NECK. YOU COULD MOUNT THE BASS AND GUITAR TO A SINGLE BODY OR EACH INDIVIDUALLY.

THE GUY WHO CAME UP WITH THIS IDEA CAME FROM NEW JERSEY AND PLAYED PRETTY GOOD GUITAR AND BASS. HIS PRO- TOTYPE WAS ROUGH BUT IT WORKED. THE WHOLE PROJECT WAS BADLY ENGINEERED. IT WAS THE BEAST AND IT WAS EVIL AND CAUSED MANY SLEEPLESS NIGHTS FOR ME. IF YOU OWN ONE

HOLD AN EXORCISM. SO MUCH FOR THE "BIKINI"

THE JACK WEBB TV SHOW "DRAGNET" TOOK PLACE IN THE COMPANY SOMETIME AFTER THE GUY WITH THE STRING TRIED TO HIEST EVERYTHING DOWN OFF THE BALCONY FROM THE SEVENTH FLOOR. THE CHICAGO OFFICE REPORTED THEY WERE RECEIVING GUITAR CASES WITH OUT THE GUITAR IN THEM. THERE WAS DRUM SETS AND OTHER INSTRUMENTS MISSING FROM INVENTORY. I GUESS THERE WAS A LOT OF MERCHANDISE MISSING FOR THE COMPANY TO HIRE THESE TWO GUYS TO INTERROGATE ALL OF THE EMPLOYEES ONE AT A TIME. THESE TWO USED THE GOOD GUY BAD GUY TECHNIQUE. I'LL CALL THEM PAT AND RAT. PAT WAS THE OBVIOUS GOOD GUY AND RAT THE (IN YOUR FACE) BAD GUY.

PAT SAID VERY SOFT AND SINCERE "DAN, WE KNOW YOU DIDN'T TAKE ANYTHING, BUT DID YOU EVER SEE ANYONE DO ANY-THING SUSPICIOUS." I SAID NO. IMMEDIATELY RAT GOT IN MY FACE AND ASKED ME (IN A NASTY TONE) IF I EVER SAW ANYONE BRING INSTRUMENTS TO THE MUSIC STORE I WAS TEACHING AT TWO NIGHTS A WEEK. APPARENTLY THEY KNEW ALL ABOUT ME. I SAID YES AND BY WHO. HE SAID "WE KNOW YOU WORK AS A GUITAR PLAYER ON WEEKENDS, WHY DO YOU NEED ALL THAT MONEY?" I SAID "THE PERSON WHO DELIVERED THE INSTRUMENTS TO THE STORE AT NIGHT IS THE SALESMAN FOR THAT ACCOUNT, HE HAS ALL THE BEST ACCOUNTS IN BROOKLYN, QUEENS, LONG ISLAND, NEW YORK, THE BRONX, AND NEW JERSEY AND IF THERE'S A STORE ON MARS IT'S HIS. HE IS ALSO THE WAREHOUSE MANAGER OF FREDS MUSIC ASSESSORY BUSINESS. HE MUST HAVE MADE MORE MONEY THAN EVEN FRED GRETSCH. I SAID "WHY DOES HE NEED

ALL THAT MONEY?" THEY LOOKED AT EACH OTHER, I YAWNED, THEY SAID "THANKS" AND I LEFT. THE WHOLE THING WAS RIDICULOUS. I UNDERSTAND THE THIEF WAS CAUGHT WITHOUT THIS TELEVISON PRODUCTION.

THE REPAIR DEPARTMENT RARELY SAW ANY OF THE CHET ATKINS MODELS. THERE IS NO DOUB'T IN MY MIND THAT CHET AT-KIN'S NAME SOLD A LOT OF GUITARS. ALSO THE QUALITY SAID A LOT ABOUT THE SALES TOO. AS CHET'S POPULARITY GREW SO DID THE SALES. JIMMY WEBSTER HAD A LOT TO DO WITH SIGN-ING HIM AS AN ENDORSER. JIMMY PROMOTED HIM AND HIS GUI-TARS AT EVERY MUSIC TRADE SHOW. THEY WORKED VERY HARD TO SELL THE CHET ATKIN'S NAME AND THE GUITARS. CHET SAID THAT AFTER THE COMPANY MOVED OUT OF BROOKLYN THE GUI-TARS WERE NEVER THE SAME. WELL ANYONE WITH HALF A BRAIN WOULD KNOW THIS. MOST OF THE FOREMAN STARTED THERE AROUND 1940 TO 1946. A LOT OF THE WORKMAN ON THE BENCHES WERE SKILLED CRAFTSMAN, ALSO THERE MANY YEARS, BEING GUIDED DAILY BY THE FOREMAN, WHAT A GREAT SITUATION FOR A COMPANY TO BE IN. THEN IN 1970 THE PIANO BUILDING PIN HEADS DECIDE TO MOVE THE COMPANY TO "BOONSVILLE" ARKANSAS AND HAVE THE "BEVERLY HILLBILLIES" STOP MILKING THE COWS AND BUILD THE PRESTIGIOUS GRETSCH GUITARS. THINK ABOUT IT! WOULD YOU DO IT? OF COURSE NOT. YOU'RE NOT A PIN HEAD. YOU'RE A GUITAR PLAYER, YOU GOT YOUR EDUCATION IN SMOKE FILLED BARS WITH GUN SHOT HOLES IN THE CEILING. YOU DON'T SIT IN YOUR OFFICE WITH ALL YOUR DEGREE'S HANGING ON THE WALL BEHIND YOU TO SHOW HOW SMART YOU ARE. YOU DIDN'T

NEED ALL THOSE DEGREE'S TO KNOW THAT TO MOVE THE COM-PANY WAS A MISTAKE. I GUESS WHEN THEY WERE IN SCHOOL THEY MISSED THE CLASS WHEN THE PROFESSOR SAID "FARMERS AND ENGINEERS DON'T BUILD GUITARS, ONLY SKILLED CRAFTSMAN DO." IF THEY DIDN'T LEARN IT IN SCHOOL THEY WERE LOST. THEY MOVED THE COMPANY BECAUSE SALES WERE DOWN. THE GUITAR BOOM WAS OVER.

WELL I GUESS THEY NEVER GOT A DEGREE IN "WHAT TO DO WHEN THE GUITAR BOOM IS OVER." WE HAD INVENTORY FOR THE FIRST TIME IN THE HISTORY OF THE COMPANY. DO I MOVE THE COMPANY AND WAIT FIVE YEARS AND MAYBE I'LL GET A GOOD GUI-TAR OR DO I GET THE SALESMAN TO DO THEIR JOB? THAT'S WHERE THE PROBLEM WAS. THE SALESMAN BECAME ORDER TAKERS, THEY MADE ALL THAT MONEY SITTING ON THEIR ASS TAKING OR-DERS ON THE PHONE. THEY DIDN'T WANT TO GO BACK TO WORK. IT WAS TIME TO GO OUT AND POUND THE PAVEMENT LIKE THEY DID BEFORE THE GUITAR BOOM.

EVEN THE CHICAGO BRANCH WOULD COMPLAIN THAT THEY WERE NEVER GETTING THEIR FAIR SHARE OF GUITARS. WHEN THE BOOM WAS OVER YOU DIDN'T HEAR FROM THEM. WHEN THEY DID CALL THEIR EXCUSE FOR SALES BEING DOWN WAS THE MARKET WAS SATURATED. IT WAS TIME FOR THE OFFICE TO DEMAND RE-SULTS FROM THE SALESMEN, BUT NO ONE DID. NO ONE KNEW HOW. EVERY ONE PAID THE PRICE.

HERE'S A STORY ABOUT A FEW GUYS CALLED ENGINEERS WHO JUST COULDN'T HEAR. FRED GRETSCH ASKED ME ONE DAY WHAT I THOUGHT WAS THE BEST SOUNDING AMPLIFIER. I TOLD

HIM "THE TWIN REVERB." AT THAT TIME EVERY ONE WAS TRYING TO MAKE SOLID STATE AMPLIFIERS. ALL OF THE SOLID STATE AMPS WERE VERY THIN SOUNDING. NONE OF THEM HAD THE SOUND OF A TUBE AMP. A FEW WEEKS LATER A PROTOTYPE ARRIVED AND FRED ASKED ME TO TRY IT. I TOLD HIM IT WAS VERY GOOD FOR A SOLID STATE AMP BUT IT DIDN'T SOUND LIKE THE TWIN REVERB. HE SAID THEY COPIED THE SOUND WAVES EXACTLY AND IT HAS TO SOUND THE SAME. I SAID IT DON'T. ONCE AGAIN MY BIG MOUTH PUT ME ON A PLANE.

I WAS ONCE AGAIN HEADED INTO THE WORLD OF THE SUITS. ONCE AGAIN I WAS SURROUNDED BY INTIMIDATING EYES TRYING TO MAKE ME SWEAT. BY NOW I HAD A LOT MORE EXPERIENCE THAN WHEN I PLAYED THE SOLID BODY GUITAR IN THE COURTROOM. THERE WAS AN EERIE FEELING ABOUT THIS WHOLE SETUP. WE WERE ON A STAGE IN AN AUDITORIUM. JIMMY WAS ALSO WITH ME, HE WASN'T THE SAME AS BEFORE. EVER SINCE THE COMPANY WAS SOLD HE DIDN'T SMILE AS MUCH AS HE DID. THE SIX SUITS HAD SET UP THE TWO AMPS SIDE BY SIDE. THEIR CLAIM WAS THEY SOUNDED THE SAME. THEY HAD THE AMPS SET UP TO A BOX THAT SWITCHED THE AMPS BACK AND FORTH BETWEEN EACH OTHER. THEY WERE REALLY READY FOR ME. JIMMY HANDED ME THE GUITAR AND SAID "THIS IS YOUR SHOW." THEY SAID THEY WANTED ME TO TELL THEM WHICH AMP THE SOUND WAS COMING THROUGH AS I PLAYED. I SAID OK AND STARTED TO PLAY. AS I PLAYED THEY STARTED SWITCHING BACK AND FORTH BETWEEN AMPS. I CALLED ONE AMP "THE TWIN" AND THE OTHER "SOLID."

AFTER A COUPLE OF MINUTES OF THIS THEY SAID TO STOP

PLAYING AND THEY HUDDLED TOGETHER LIKE A FOOTBALL TEAM
TO DISCUSS THE NEXT PLAY. THEY CAME OUT OF THE HUDDLE AND
ASKED ME TO TURN AROUND AND PLAY NOT FACING THE AMPS. I
KNEW I CALLED EVERY THING RIGHT BECAUSE I HEARD THE DIF-
FERENCE. I STARTED TO PLAY AGAIN WITH THE AMPS BEHIND ME,
THEY STARTED SWITCHING BACK AND FORTH BETWEEN AMPS. I
STARTED TO CALL OUT "THE TWIN" OR "SOLID." FOR SOME REASON
I COULD HEAR THE DIFFERENCE BETWEEN THE TWO AMPS BETTER
WITH THEM BEHIND ME. EVENTUALLY THEY SAID TO STOP PLAYING.
THEY AGREED THAT I HEARD THE DIFFERENCE BETWEEN THE TWO
AMPS BUT THEY STILL DIDN'T UNDERSTAND IT. THEY THEN TOOK
US OUT TO LUNCH AND WE DISCUSSED DIFFERENT SUBJECTS.
NO ONE MENTIONED THEIR TAKING OVER THE GRETSCH COMPA-
NY. THEY MUST HAVE KNOWN THAT WE WERE NOT HAPPY ABOUT
THAT.

AFTER LUNCH THEY ASKED ME TO PLAY AGAIN. THEY WANTED
TO TAKE SOME READINGS WHILE I PLAYED. THEY WANTED ME TO
PLAY WITH A FORCEFUL ATTACK WITH THE PICK AND THEN A LIGHT
ATTACK. I DID THIS FOR AWHILE UNTIL THEY SAID TO STOP. THEY
SAID THEY WOULD HAVE TO MAKE SOME ADJUSTMENTS WITH THE
AMP. I DON'T KNOW WHAT HAPPENED AFTER THAT BECAUSE THE
FACTORY MOVED AND I WAS GONE.

SOME TIME AROUND 1967 THE UNION DECIDED TO STRIKE.
THEY WERE OUT FOR ABOUT THREE MONTHS. I THINK THIS ACTU-
ALLY WORKED IN FAVOR OF THE COMPANY. SALES WERE DOWN,
THE SALESMAN WERE STILL ASLEEP, AND WE HAD A FEW HUNDRED
GUITARS IN INVENTORY. THE FOREMAN WERE MADE TO WORK

NIGHTS IN THE OTHER GRETSCH BUILDING A FEW BLOCKS AWAY. THIS BUILDING MADE GRETSCH DRUMS. THESE INSTRUMENTS WERE ALSO CONSIDERED THE BEST. THE FOREMAN MADE DRUMS, FILLED THE ORDERS AND SENT THEM OUT. THE STRIKE WAS NOT WITHOUT INCIDENT. ONE FOREMAN HAD HIS SHARE OF FLATS AND A WINDOW BROKEN ON HIS CAR. HE ALSO HAD ABOUT TWENTY POUNDS OF DOGGIE POO ALL OVER HIS CAR. TO THIS DAY I CAN STILL PICTURE THESE PEOPLE HUNTING FOR DOGGIE POO ALL OVER BROOKLYN. ONE OF THE HUNTERS LATER TOLD ME THAT HIS TECHNIQUE WAS TO FOLLOW SOMEONE WALKING THEIR DOG. WHEN THEY STOPPED HE STOPPED. HE SAID HE LEARNED TO HAVE A LOT OF PATIENCE ON THIS PARTICULAR MISSION. WHEN THE DOG SQUATTED HE SAID HE KNEW HE WAS GOING MAKE A SCORE. ALL HE HAD TO DO WAS GO UP TO THE PERSON AND ASK THEM IF HE COULD HAVE THE POO. HE SAID THEY USUALLY LOOKED AT HIM STRANGE AND WANTED TO KNOW WHAT HE WANTED THE BAG OF POO FOR. HE SAID HIS WIFE USED IT IN HER GARDEN. HE SAID THEY USUALLY HANDED HIM THE BAG OF GOLD AND WALKED AWAY VERY QUICKLY DRAGGING THEIR DOG WITH THEM. HE TOLD ME HE LIKED FOLLOWING THE PEOPLE WHO WEREN'T CARRYING THE SMALL DOGGIE SHOVEL AND BAG. HE KNEW THEY WERE GOING TO LITTER, BUT AT LEAST HE DIDN'T HAVE TO EXPLAIN HIS WANT-ING THE DEPOSIT. THIS WENT ON FOR DAYS HE SAID UNTIL HE GOT ARRESTED. HE SAID A WOMAN HE WAS FOLLOWING STARTED SCREAMING AND THE POLICE WERE NEARBY AND GRABBED HIM. HE EXPLAINED TO THEM THAT ALL HE WANTED WAS THE DOGGIE POO AND HANDED THEM THE BAG TO SHOW THEM. AFTER THEY

LOOKED INSIDE THE BAG AND SHOOK THEIR HEADS IN DISBELIEF THEY THREW IT DOWN A NEARBY SEWER. THEY CALLED HIS WIFE TO COME DOWN TO THE STATION HOUSE AND GET HIM. SHE EX-PLAINED ABOUT THE STRIKE. THEY TOLD HER TO TAKE HIM HOME AND KEEP HIM OUT OF TROUBLE. THE DESK SERGEANT SAID HE SHOULD GET A JOB WITH THE DEPARTMENT OF SANITATION WITH HIS SKILLS AT COLLECTING.

WHEN GEORGE HARRISON FIRST APPEARED ON NATIONAL TELEVISION PLAYING HIS GRETSCH CHET ATKINS "COUNTRY GEN-TLEMAN" GUITAR LETTERS STARTED TO COME IN BY THE SACK FULL. THE OFFICE PEOPLE HAD TO WORK SATURDAYS JUST TO OPEN IT. THERE WAS SO MUCH MAIL IT HAD TO BE SEPARATED INTO CATEGORIES TO BE READ AND ANSWERED. REQUESTS FOR CATA-LOGS MUST HAVE PUT A SMILE ON THE PRINTER'S FACE. SOME WANTED TO KNOW WHERE TO GO TO BUY A GRETSCH CHET AT-KINS GUITAR AS THEIR LOCAL MUSIC STORE WAS OUT OF STOCK. PEOPLE CAME TO NEW YORK TO BUY GUITARS. THEY CAME FROM ALL OVER THEY CALLED THE FACTORY ASKING FOR TOURS OF THE FACTORY. I BECAME A TOUR GUIDE. THEY ASKED ME ALL KINDS OF QUESTIONS ABOUT CHET ATKINS AND HARRISON.

MANY WANTED TO KNOW IF WE GAVE THE "COUNTRY GENTLE-MAN" GUITAR TO HIM. I TOLD THEM HE BOUGHT IT IN ENGLAND AND HE WAS A GREAT FAN OF CHET ATKINS AND HE WANTED THE COUN-TRY GENTLEMAN GUITAR. THEY WANTED TO KNOW IF HARRISON'S PLAYING THE GRETSCH GUITAR INCREASED SALES AND I TOLD THEM YES, BUT IF HE WASN'T A FAN OF CHET ATKINS HE PROBABLY WOULDN'T HAVE BOUGHT THE GUITAR. WHO WAS RESPONSIBLE

FOR THE SALES? I'D HAVE TO SAY CHET ATKINS. BUT IF HARRISON WASN'T SEEN ON T.V. WITH IT WHO WOULD IT BE? AND AROUND AND AROUND WE GO! JUST REMEMBER THAT AFTER ALL WAS SAID AND DONE ABOUT WHO OR WHAT CAUSED THE GROWTH OF SALES ONLY ONE PERSON SMILED ALL THE WAY TO THE BANK.

GETTING BACK TO THE GUITAR BOOM, PLAYERS WERE COMING UP TO NEW YORK FROM DOWN SOUTH AND SLEEPING IN THEIR CARS AND VANS JUST TO GET THE WELL KNOWN 48TH ST. DISCOUNT ON THEIR PURCHASE OF A GRETSCH GUITAR. AS THE BOOM WENT ON THE DISCOUNTS GOT LESS AND LESS. THE STORES WERE CHARGING NEAR THE LIST PRICE. THE STORES WERE ASKING FOR FASTER AND FASTER DELIVERY. THEY SAID THEY WOULD FINISH THE GUITAR THEMSELVES, JUST SEND THE GUITAR BODY WITH THE NECK ON IT. NATURALLY WE DIDN'T. ALL THIS MADNESS OVER GUITARS WAS UNBELIEVABLE. I SURE MISSED THE QUIET DAYS OF THE LATE FIFTIES WITH JUST TEN GUITARS A DAY, LITTLE DID I KNOW THOSE DAYS WERE RETURNING.

GOING BACK TO THE GOOD YEAR OF 1957, NEXT TO THE REPAIR DEPARTMENT WAS THE MACHINE SHOP. THE FOREMAN WAS SID LAKEN. HE WAS ONE OF THOSE GUYS WITH ALL THOSE DEGREES HANGING ON THE WALL BEHIND HIS DESK. HIS COLLECTION KEPT GROWING. I DIDN'T KNOW IF HE WAS GOING TO SCHOOL OR A PRINTER.

HE WAS A VERY GOOD MACHINIST AND DID A GOOD JOB. IN THE SIXTIES HE WAS MOVED TO THE FACTORY OFFICE AND PUT IN CHARGE OF THE TIME STUDY OPERATION. PIECE WORK WAS INTRODUCED AND SID WAS IN CHARGE OF TIMING ALL THE DIFFER-

ENT OPERATIONS. AT FIRST IT WAS A DISASTER. SOME JOBS WERE TIMED SO BADLY THAT THE WORKER WENT OVER HIS QUOTER IN HALF A DAY, HIS PAY CHECKS WERE HUGE. QUALITY TOOK A STEP BACK ALSO. AFTER A LOT OF WORK RETIMING THE DIFFERENT JOBS THINGS WORKED OUT. THE WORKERS WERE BEING PAID A FAIR WAGE FOR THEIR LABOR AND THE FACTORY ALSO BENEFITED. THIS METHOD HELPED CONTROL COST AND PRICING.

THE MACHINE SHOP MADE MOST OF THE METAL PARTS FOR THE GUITARS AND DRUMS. NEXT TO THE MACHINE SHOP WAS THE PLATING DEPARTMENT WHERE THE METAL PARTS RECEIVED THEIR THIN COATING OF GOLD OR CHROME PLATING. NOTHING INTERESTING EVER HAPPENED IN THESE TWO DEPARTMENTS BECAUSE THEY WEREN'T DEALING WITH THE WOODEN PARTS OF THE GUITAR.

MY ASSOCIATION WITH THE "7" STRING GUITAR GENIUS "GEORGE VAN EPPS" WAS A PRIVILEGE. TO TALK TO HIM ABOUT GUITARS, MUSIC AND OTHER SUBJECTS WAS ALWAYS A MAIN EVENT IN MY LIFE. HE ALWAYS GAVE ME TIPS ON PLAYING THE "7" STRING GUITAR. WHEN WE SAT ONE ON ONE VERY EARLY IN THE MORNING AT THE NAMM SHOWS HE WOULD SHOW ME DIFFERENT WAYS OF PLAYING ARRANGEMENTS OF SONGS I WORKED OUT. I WOULD PLAY AND HE WOULD STOP ME AT CERTAIN PARTS AND SAY "THAT'S GREAT DAN NOW TRY IT LIKE THIS." WHEN HE SHOWED ME HOW HE DID IT I ALMOST FELL OFF THE CHAIR. SOME OF THE THINGS HE SHOWED ME WERE REAL FINGER TWISTERS. THIS MAN WAS SO HUMBLE AND SINCERE IT WAS OVERWHELMING. HE SENT ME A CHRISTMAS CARD ONCE. I COULDN'T BELIEVE IT. I WENT TO SEE

HIM PLAY IN NEW YORK CITY EVERY TIME HE MADE A RARE AP-
PEARANCE THERE. ONE TIME WHEN I WENT TO SEE HIM PLAY HE
CAME RIGHT OVER TO ME, SHOOK MY HAND AND SAID "HI DAN, ITS
GREAT TO SEE YOU."

GEORGE WENT ON TO SAY THAT HE WAS REALLY HAPPY
THAT I WAS THERE TO SEE HIM, AND HEAR HIM PLAY. IN OUR CON-
SERVATION HE SAID "AT LEAST I KNOW ONE PERSON IS HERE TO
LISTEN TO ME PLAY AND NOT HERE TO COUNT THE MISTAKES I
MAKE." MAYBE HE KNEW THAT THE MAJORITY OF THE AUDIENCE
WAS GUITAR PLAYERS AND SOME HAD SUCH LARGE EGOS THAT
EVERY SLIGHT BLUNDER IN HIS TECHNIQUE PACIFIED THEM. WELL
THEY DIDN'T GET THEIR EGOS SATISIFIED THAT NIGHT. HIS PLAY-
ING WAS OUTSTANDING AND TECHNIQUE FLAWLESS. TO PERFORM
IN FRONT OF SUCH AN AUDIENCE HAD TO BE SUPER PRESSURE.
EVERY GUITAR PLAYER WHO COULD POSSIBLY BE THERE WOULD
SHOW UP EVENTUALLY. GEORGE WAS THE ONLY GUITAR PLAYER
WHO USED HEAVY GAUGE STRINGS ON HIS GUITAR AND NOT GET
FINGER NOISE. I ASKED HIM HOW HE DID THIS AND HE SAID YOU
LIFT YOUR FINGERS UP OFF ONE NOTE AND DOWN ON THE NEXT
NOTE WITH OUT SLIDING TO IT. NEVER SLIDE FROM NOTE TO NOTE
UNLESS YOU WANT THAT SLURRING EFFECT. THIS TAKES A LOT OF
PRACTICE.

GEORGE WOULD ALWAYS PLAY AT THE NAMM (NATIONAL AS-
SOCIATION OF MUSIC MERCHANTS.) CONVENTION. THIS IS A TRADE
SHOW WHERE ALL THE MANUFACTURERS RENT A SPACE IN A CON-
VENTION HALL AND DISPLAY ALL THEIR MUSICAL INSTRUMENTS.
THEY USUALLY HAVE THE ARTISTS WHO ENDORSE THEIR INSTRU-

MENTS PLAY. GEORGE WOULD PLAY HIS GRETSCH "7" STRING GUI-
TAR TO ABSOLUTE PERFECTION. EVERY TIME HE PLAYED I WAS
THERE LISTENING, WATCHING AND WONDERING HOW HE MAS-
TERED THIS FINGERSTYLE METHOD OF PLAYING "WALKING BASS,
CHORD AND MELODY AT THE SAME TIME WITH SUCH PROFOUND
EFFICIENCY. I HAVE HEARD MANY GUYS PLAY THIS STYLE. THEY
WERE VERY GOOD BUT THEY NEVER CAME UP TO GEORGE. I RE-
MEMBER ONE GUY COMING UP TO GEORGE WITH AN ACOUSTIC
GUITAR. HE WAS TELLING GEORGE TO LISTEN TO HIM PLAY "SATIN
DOLL" JUST THE WAY HE DOES BY TUNING THE GUITAR DIFFER-
ENT.HE PLAYED THE FIRST EIGHT BARS AND IT SOUNDED LIKE THE
CHORD CHANGES GEORGE USED. GEORGE TOLD HIM THAT HE
SOUNDED GREAT BUT IT WAS EASIER TO DO IT WITH NORMAL TUN-
ING AND HE PROCEEDED TO SHOW HIM. THE GUY SAID HE LIKED
HIS WAY BETTER AND WALKED AWAY. GEORGE JUST LOOKED AT
ME AND SMILED. HE TOLD ME THAT OTHER THAN TUNING THE SIX
STRING DOWN TO "D" HE DIDN'T LIKE ALTERED TUNINGS AS THEY
GET INTO BAD HABITS.

MOST PLAYERS THAT I KNOW OF WHO PLAY THIS STYLE USU-
ALLY CAN MAKE A NICE ARRANGEMENT OF THE MAIN MELODY BUT
WHEN ITS TIME TO TAKE A SOLO THEY CANT KEEP THE BASS LINE
GOING BEHIND THE IMPROVISED LINE THEY ARE PLAYING.

CHET ATKINS ANOTHER PLAYERS PLAYER ALSO ADMIRED
GEORGES PLAYING. I REMEMBER ONE TIME AT A NAMM CONVEN-
TION GEORGE WAS PLAYING. CHET, JIMMY WEBSTER AND I WERE
STANDING IN THE BACK OF THE ROOM WATCHING. CHETS EYES
WERE FIXED ON GEORGE.

HE WAS HAVING ONE OF HIS SUPER PLAYING DAYS AND EV-ERYONE WAS IN AWE OF HIM. ALL OF A SUDDEN GEORGE MADE A SPECTACULAR MOVE IN THE PIECE HE WAS PERFORMING, CHETS MOUTH OPENED WIDE AND HIS CIGAR FELL TO THE FLOOR. HE WAS SUPPOSED TO PLAY NEXT. HE DIDN'T. GEORGE IS A TOUGH ACT TO FOLLOW. HE TOLD JIMMY "I'LL PLAY LATER." EVERYONE WAS DISAP-POINTED THAT CHET DIDN'T PLAY. HE PLAYED LATER AND WOWED THEM.

I REMEMBER THE BROTHERS "LOS INDIOS TRABAJARIES" HAD NO TROUBLE FOLLOWING GEORGE. THEY HAD A HIT RECORD AT THE TIME "MARIA–ELENA." THEY BOTH PLAYED WHITE FALCONS. ON ONE OF THE WHITE FALCONS WE HAD TO INSTALL AN EXTRA FRET UNDER THE FIRST STRING NEAR THE BRIDGE. I REALLY CAN'T REMEMBER HOW WE DID THIS, BUT I THINK IT WAS ATTACHED TO AN EXTENSION ATTACHED TO THE PICK GUARD. I DON'T REMEM-BER IF IT WAS SILVER OR GOLD, BUT I WAS TOLD IT WAS ONE OF HIS TEETH. FORGIVE ME IF I WAS MISINFORMED BUT IT SOUNDED WEIRD BACK THEN AND IT STILL SOUNDS WEIRD.

WHEN WE MADE "BO DIDLEYS" GUITAR I THOUGHT "WOW" ANOTHER WEIRDO. WHEN I SAT DOWN TO TEST IT, IT WAS VERY UNCOMFORTABLE. I PUT A STRAP ON IT AND PLAYED IT STANDING UP. IT PLAYED VERY WELL. I DIDN'T REALIZE AT THE TIME I MIGHT BE THE ONLY ONE TO EVER ACTUALLY PLAY THE GUITAR UNLESS SOMEONE ELSE WOULD PICK IT UP.WHEN I SAW HIM PERFORM HE DIDN'T PLAY IT IN A MELODIC SENSE. HE JUST STRUMMED THESE DAMPENED RHYTHMS WHILE HE SANG. WEIRD OR EXTRAORDI-NARY I STILL DON'T KNOW.

I REMEMBER A BLACK FALCON, A GREEN FALCON AND YOU SHOULD HAVE SEEN THE RED FALCON, IT HURT MY EYES. THE YELLOW FALCON GOT THE AWARD FOR "GAUDY." SOME PLAYERS HAD THEIR NAMES INLAID ON THE FINGER BOARD WITH MOTHER OF PEARL LETTERS.

ONCE AN ORDER CAME IN FROM A STORE FOR AN ALL BLACK SAL SALVADOR GUITAR MODEL # 6199. HIS CUSTOMER WANTED TWENTY FIVE COATS OF LACQUER ON IT. THE OFFICE TOLD HIM THAT FOUR OR FIVE COATS IS THE MOST YOU CAN DO. ANY MORE AND THE LACQUER WOULD CRACK. THE STORE SAID TO DO IT THE NORMAL WAY. WHEN THE GUITAR WAS READY THE OWNER OF THE STORE SAID THAT HIS CUSTOMER WOULD PICK UP THE GUITAR. WHEN HE CAME TO THE FACTORY HE ASKED FOR ME. WHEN HE PICKED UP THE GUITAR AND LOOKED AT IT HE STARTED YELLING AND SCREAMING "THIS ISN'T TWENTY FIVE COATS OF PAINT" OVER AND OVER AGAIN. THIS GUY WAS TOTALLY OUT OF CONTOL. I GUESS THE STORE OWNER DIDN'T TELL HIM THAT WE COULDN'T HONOR HIS REQUEST. AFTER A LONG PERIOD OF THIS RANTING AND RAVING HE PUT THE GUITAR DOWN AND STORMED OUT MUMBLING TO HIMSELF. I SHOULD HAVE TOLD HIM TO TAKE THE GUITAR TO "EARL SCHIEB" THE AUTO PAINTER, HE DID CARS BACK THEN FOR$29.99 HOW DID HE KNOW THERE WASN'T 25 COATS OF LACQUER ON THE GUITAR.? MAYBE IT WOULD HAVE BEEN TWICE ITS SIZE. I WISH WE DID IT.

ONE TIME AT A NAMM CONVENTION I HAD TO GO TO A BREAKFAST WITH JIMMY WEBSTER. IT HAD SOMETHING TO DO WITH COUNTRY MUSIC AWARDS I THINK. IT WAS AT TEN O'CLOCK IN THE

MORNING AND REPRESENTATIVES OF EACH COMPANY WERE IN-VITED TO ATTEND.

"JOHNNY CASH" AND HIS BAND WERE THERE. I AM NOT A COUNTRY MUSIC FAN. I DON'T DISLIKE IT, I JUST LIKE STRAIGHT AHEAD JAZZ. NOW REMEMBER, IT WAS TEN O'CLOCK IN THE MORN-ING AND THE WHOLE AUDITORIUM WAS PACKED. SUDDENLY THE WHOLE PLACE GOES DARK AND A DEEP VOICE SAYS. "HI, I'M JOHN-NY CASH." THE SPOTLIGHT OPENS ON THE "MAN IN BLACK" ON STAGE. THE WHOLE PLACE EXPLODES WITH SCREAMS AND THUN-DERING APPLAUSE ALL AROUND ME. THE BAND STARTED PLAYING. THE GUITAR STARTED PLAYING THAT SIGNATURE STRING MUTED VAMP. JOHNNY STARTED TO SING AND AGAIN THE EXPLOSION OF CHEERS AND APPLAUSE AND THEN A SUDDEN SILENCE AS THEY FIXED THEMSELVES IN A STATE OF REVERENCE TOWARD THE STAGE AND THE "MAN IN BLACK".

I STOOD THERE LOOKING AROUND AT ALL THE PEOPLE WITH THEIR MIXED EMOTIONS. SOME HAD BLANK EXPRESSIONS ON THEIR FACES WITH THEIR MOUTHS OPEN, SOME WERE SMILING AND THE ONES WHO WERE CRYING I THOUGHT "HOW REDICU-LOUS".

I STOOD THERE LISTENING TO SONG AFTER SONG AND START-ED TO GET CAUGHT UP IN THE CHARISMA OF THE "MAN IN BLACK" I LISTENED TO THE WORDS HE SANG AND THE STORIES THEY TOLD. I GOT CAUGHT UP IN THIS MOMENT OF TOTAL REVERENCE WITH EVERYONE ELSE. I WALKED OUT OF THAT BREAKFAST VERY RE-LAXED AND KIND OF HIGH ON LIFE. I SPOKE TO HIM VERY BRIEFLY LATER THAT DAY. HE WAS VERY SINCERE THE WAY HE SPOKE, JUST

LIKE THE SONGS HE WRITES AND PERFORMS. IT SADDENED ME A GREAT DEAL WHEN HE GOT SICK AND EVENTUALLY PASSED AWAY. HE LEFT HIS MUSICAL MARK ON THIS WORLD WITH HIS SONGS THAT YOU STILL HEAR TODAY.

I MET LUIS BONFA' WHEN I WORKED FOR THE ONE "THOUSAND DOLLAR MAN." HE DRESSED LIKE A FARMER. HE WORE THOSE ONE PIECE DUNGEREES WITH THE STRAPS OVER THE SHOULDERS. I THOUGHT HE LOOKED VERY COOL.HE WAS THE ORIGINATOR OF THE "BOSSA NOVA" RHYTHM. HE WROTE THE TUNE "A DAY IN THE LIFE OF A FOOL." THIS TUNE IS IN EVERY JAZZ MUSICIANS BOOK. THEY ALSO USED THS TUNE FOR THE MOVIE "BLACK ORPHEUS." THE ONE THOUSAND DOLLAR MAN INTRODUCED HIM TO ME SAYING "THIS IS DAN DUFFY HE WORKED FOR GRETSCH GUITARS FOR MANY YEARS AND HE CAN FIX YOUR GUITAR." I IMMEDIATELY TOOK A DEEP BREATH AND SAID TO MYSELF "OH GOD HELP ME." I SHOOK HIS HAND AND TOLD HIM HOW MUCH I ENJOY HIS PLAYING AND THE MUSIC HE WRITES. HE SAID HE NEEDS TO GET ANOTHER HIT LIKE THE THEME FOR THE MOVIE "BLACK ORPHUES" SO HE CAN GO BACK TO JUST FISHING.I TOLD HIM THAT I GO FISHING EVERY CHANCE THAT I GET, WITH THIS WE STARTED TALKING ABOUT FISHING. WHILE WE WERE TALKING I COULD SEE THAT THE ONE THOUSAND DOLLAR MAN WAS GETTING NERVOUS. THIS IDLE CHATTER WAS COSTING HIM MONEY. ANYWAY, LUIS TOLD ME THAT THE FRETS ON HIS GUITAR WERE TOO HIGH AND WAS HARD TO PLAY. IT WAS ONE OF THOSE BEAUTIFUL FLAMED ROSEWOOD GUITARS FROM BRAZIL. TO BAD THESE GUITARS HAD SUCH A MOISTURE PROBLEM. WHEN HE SAID THAT THE FRETS WERE TOO HIGH I IM-

MEDIATELY THOUGHT OF SAL SALVADOR. CARMINE USED TO LEVEL THE FRETS ON HIS GUITARS ALL THE WAY DOWN AND THEN ROUND THEM OFF. WHEN YOUR DONE WITH THE FILES YOU HAVE TO USE VARIOUS GRADES OF SANDPAPER AND WORK ON ONE FRET AT A TIME BRINGING IT TO A BRILLIANT SHINE AND A SMOOTHE GLASS LIKE FINISH. YOU HAVE TO TAKE YOUR TIME DOING THIS. YOU HAVE TO BE VERY CAREFUL ROUNDING OFF THE ENDS OF THE FRETS BECAUSE THERE ISNT MUCH MEAT LEFT ON THE FRET ITSELF. IF YOU TAKE OFF TO MUCH YOU WILL HAVE A SHORT FRET. THIS FRET WILL POP UP AND CAUSE A BUZZ. NO GLUE WILL HOLD IT DOWN. IT MIGHT HOLD FOR A WHILE BUT EVENTUALLY IT WILL POP UP. REPLACING ONE FRET IS KIND OF HARD. YOU USUALLY HAVE TO REPLACE ALL THE FRETS. ALL MY GUITARS WERE DONE THIS WAY BY CARMINE.

I COULD SEE THAT THE ONE THOUSAND DOLLAR MAN WAS GETTING VERY NERVOUS AND ABOUT TO JUMP OUT OF HIS MONEY BELT. TO EASE HIS PAIN I TOLD HIM I WAS ALMOST DONE. AS I WAS TESTING THE GUITAR LUIS CAME OUT OF THE OFFICE AND WALKED OVER TO ME.I STOPPED PLAYING AND HANDED THE GUITAR TO HIM. I TOOK HIM TO THE SHOW ROOM WHERE ALL THE INSTRUMENTS WERE ON DISPLAY. IT WAS VERY QUIET THERE. HE SAT DOWN AND PLAYED THE GUITAR. HE PLAYED FOR QUITE AWHILE. HE KEPT NODDING HIS HEAD WITH APPROVAL AS HE PLAYED. HE EVENTUALLY SAID THE GUITAR PLAYED TERRIFIC. THE ONE THOUSAND DOLLAR MAN SMILED, I SHOOK HANDS WITH LUIS, HE COULDN'T THANK ME ENOUGH. I SAID GOODBYE AND WENT BACK TO WORK. THE ONE THOUSAND DOLLAR MAN WAS RELIEVED.

BACK IN THE REPAIR DEPARTMENT AT 60 BROADWAY, BROOK-
LYN, AROUND THE GOOD YEAR OF 1963, CARMINE WAS TRYING TO
SOLVE THE MYSTERY OF THE WEAK SOUNDING PICKUP. THE GUI-
TAR CAME BACK FOR A REFINISH AND NEW PICKUPS. WE GOT A LOT
OF REFINISH JOBS DURING THE GUITAR BOOM. GUYS WERE PICK-
ING UP THEIR GUITARS AGAIN AND IT WAS CHEAPER TO TAKE THIS
ROUTE. I TOLD CARMINE THAT I KNEW WHAT WAS CAUSING THE
PROBLEM. THE PEOPLE DOWN STAIRS WHO MAKE THE PICKUPS
WERE PUTTING THE MAGNETS IN TURNED AROUND. THIS CAUSED
THE PICKUPS TO BE OUT OF PHASE. THE POLARITY WAS OFF GIV-
ING THE GUITAR A VERY DIFFERENT SOUND WHEN BOTH PICKUPS
WERE ON AT THE SAME TIME. YOU HAD TO RAISE THE VOLUME TO
HEAR IT. LATER THIS SOUND WOULD BE PERFECTED ELECTRONI-
CALLY AND OFTEN USED. OUT OF PHASE BECAME AN ACCEPTED
SOUND IN LATER YEARS AND HERE I WAS FIXING IT. JUST LIKE THE
AMPS WE WERE MAKING. WE WERE TRYING TO MAKE AN AMP THAT
PLAYED AT A HIGH LEVEL WITHOUT DISTORTING.

THIS WAS A NEVER ENDING QUEST. LOUD AND CLEAN IS WHAT
WE WANTED. THIS PROBLEM WAS EVENTUALLY SOLVED BY THE
DISTORTION PEDAL. CAN YOU BELIEVE IT? ALL THE YEARS TRYING
TO PERFECT A CLEAN SOUNDING AMP AND THEY KILL IT WITH A
PEDAL. THE ACCEPTED SOUND WAS NOW LOUD AND DISTORTED.
THE AMPS NOW HAD TO BE BIG ALSO. SOME WERE LARGE ENOUGH
TO STAND IN. ONE HAD CUSHIONED VINYL COVERING. I GUESS
IT HAD TO BE CUSHIONED IN CASE THE FIVE GUYS WHO WERE
CARRYING IT TO THE GIG FOR YOU DROPPED IT. THIS AMP WAS
REALLY A DUMB LOOKING THING. IT BELONGS IN THE SAME CAT-

EGORY WITH THE PADDED GUITAR. THEY WOULD LOOK GOOD SIDE BY SIDE. DUMB AND DUMBER. ONE SERIOUS NOTE AT THIS TIME, I WONDER WHERE THE PADDED GUITARS ARE? THERE WAS TWO. ONE WAS GREEN AND THE OTHER WAS TAN. DON'T FORGET THEY LOOK LIKE CAR SEATS OR A SKI JACKET.

ABOUT A MONTH LATER THINGS WOULD TAKE A DRAMATIC TURN. I HEARD THIS GUITAR BEING BANGED ON OUT SIDE THE FACTORY OFFICE. NOT BEING PLAYED, JUST BEING STRUMMED OPEN STRINGS AND LOUD AS HELL. I WALKED DOWN TO THE OFFICE TO SEE WHO WAS GIVING EVERYONE A HEADACHE. FRED GRETSCH WAS THERE TRYING TO TALK TO THIS GUY OVER THE NOISE THIS LITTLE RED HEADED KID WITH FRECKLES WAS MAKING. THE KID LOOKED LIKE HE BELONGED ON THE COVER OF "MAD MAGAZINE." YOU KNOW, THE KID WHO SAYS "WHAT ME WORRY?" THE KID KNEW HE WAS ANNOYING ME BUT HE KEPT BANGING AWAY AT THE GUITAR. THE OLDER GUY WAS TELLING FRED THAT THE TREND NOW WAS SMALL AMPS THAT PLAYED LOUD. "HERE WE GO AGAIN" I THOUGHT.

FRED ASKED ME WHAT I THOUGHT, I SAID I DON'T KNOW BUT I WOULD GET JIMMY WEBSTER. I WASN'T GOING TO LET JIMMY GET AWAY WITHOUT CATCHING THIS KIDS ACT.

JIMMY CAME INTO THE FACTORY WITH THAT STINKING PIPE CLENCHED BETWEEN HIS TEETH AND LOOKED AT THE "WHAT ME WORRY KID" WACKING AWAY AT HIS CRAPPY GUITAR SHOWING HOW LOUD THE AMP WAS. JIMMY WALKED RIGHT OVER TO THE KID, PUT HIS HAND ON THE GUITAR AND SAID "OKAY, OKAY WE ALL KNOW YOU CANT PLAY" THEN HE LOOKED AT ME, I WAS LAUGHING

LIKE CRAZY. I STARTED TO WALK AWAY AND THE KID STARTED TO BANG ON THE GUITAR, JIMMY TURNED AROUND AND LOOKED AT HIM AND HE STOPPED. I WALKED AWAY STILL LAUGHING AND THAT WAS THE BEGINNING OF THE NEXT BIG CHANGE IN AMPS.

YESTERDAY 5/28/05 I DECIDED TO TAKE A RIDE TO THE GRETSCH FACTORY IN BROOKLYN. I HAVEN'T BEEN THERE IN 35 YEARS. I WANTED TO TAKE SOME PICTURES OF THE BUILDING. I WAS TOLD THAT IT WAS MADE INTO VERY EXPENSIVE CONDOS. MY WIFE PAT CAME WITH ME TO TAKE THE PICTURES. I DID THE POSING AND MY TWO SONS BRIAN AND JOE DID THE DIRECTING. MY SONS STILL LIVE IN MASPETH WHERE I GREW UP. ITS ON THE QUEENS, BROOKLYN BORDER LINE AND IS ABOUT 10 MILES FROM THE GRETSCH BUILDING. MY SON BRIAN DROVE SO I COULD CHECK OUT THE BROOKLYN AREA THAT I HADN'T SEEN FOR A LONG TIME.I COULDN'T BELIEVE HOW MUCH THE AREA CHANGED. THE STREETS WERE ACTUALLY CLEAN. THERE IS A SMALL RESTAURANT ACROSS THE STREET FROM THE BUILDING WITH AN OUTSIDE DINING AREA. THE ONLY OUTSIDE DINING I EVER SAW WAS A GUY PUSHING A FRANKFURTER CART. I SAW A POLICEMAN WALKING A BEAT. I NEVER SAW THAT DOWN THERE, THEY WERE USUALLY TWO TO A CAR.

THE GRETSCH BUILDING WAS RESTORED INSIDE AND OUT. IT LOOKS REALLY GOOD. THE CONDOS ARE VERY EXPENSIVE. I READ IN THE PAPER THAT ONE SOLD FOR $350, 000. IT WAS 700 SQUARE FEET. I DON'T KNOW WHO OWNS THE BUILDING NOW. I ASKED THE SECURITY GUARD IF I COULD GO INSIDE AND HE SAID HE WAS ON A BREAK. THAT'S THE NICE WAY OF SAYING NO. THE GLASS ENTRANCE IN FRONT AND BACK ARE LOCKED. THE SECURI-

TY GUARDS LET YOU IN WITH PROPER I. D. I'M SURE THE TENANTS ARE HAUNTED BY THE FAINT SOUND OF THE GRETSCH GUITARS PLAYING THE "FRED GRETSCH BLUES." IT WAS A GOOD DAY FOR ME. A DAY OF MIXED EMOTIONS, BUT A GOOD DAY.

THE PICTURE OF ME STANDING IN FRONT OF THE BUILDING WITH THE GRAFFITI ALL OVER IT IS WHATS LEFT OF "RED'S" BAR. RED QUIT GRETSCH WHEN THE PIANO GUYS TOOK OVER THE COMPANY. HE JUST SAID "I'M OUTTA HERE." RED WORKED THERE SINCE HIGH SCHOOL. HE BOUGHT THE BAR BUT IT ONLY LASTED A FEW YEARS.FRED, RED AND MYSELF HUNG OUT HERE EVERY CHANCE WE HAD. EVERY TIME I TALKED TO THEM WE WOULD REMINISCE ABOUT THOSE GREAT TIMES.

THE GREEN OK CARD FOLLOWED ME WHERE EVER I WENT. IN 1980, TEN YEARS AFTER MY TOUR OF DUTY WITH THE GRETSCH COMPANY, I GOT SICK. I WAS IN THE HOSPITAL FOR A FEW WEEKS. WHILE I WAS THERE I MET THIS HOSPITAL ATTENDANT WHO WORKED THE NIGHT SHIFT. AFTER A WEEK I STARTED TO FEEL BETTER SO I SPENT MOST OF MY NIGHTS IN THE VISITORS ROOM. I WAS NEVER A GOOD SLEEPER. THE ATTENDANT BROUGHT ME COFFEE EVERY NIGHT AND WE WOULD SIT AND TALK. HE TOLD ME HE PLAYED THE GUITAR AND THAT HE HAD A GRETSCH CHET ATKINS MODEL GUITAR. WHEN I TOLD HIM THAT I PLAYED THE GUITAR AND SIGNED THE GREEN OK CARD THAT HUNG ON THE GUITAR WHEN HE BOUGHT IT HE FLIPPED OUT. THE NEXT NIGHT HE BROUGHT IN HIS GUITAR. THE PIECE WAS FIFTEEN YEARS OLD AND WAS IN GREAT SHAPE. WHEN HE OPENED THE CASE HE HAD THE BODY INSIDE A TEESHIRT AND THE NECK WAS WRAPPED IN THE POLISHING

CLOTH THAT CAME WITH THE GUITAR. THESE WERE ALL THE SIGNS THAT I KNEW HE CARED FOR HIS INSTRUMENT. I PICKED UP THE GUITAR AND PLAYED IT. THE GUITAR NEEDED A NECK ADJUSTMENT SO I TOLD HIM TO BRING THE RIGHT HEX WRENCH SO I COULD ADJUST IT. I FIXED THE NECK THE NEXT NIGHT AND WE BOTH SPENT TIME PLAYING THE GUITAR AND TALKING. HE TOLD ME ABOUT A LOT OF STRANGE DISEASES HE SEEN WORKING AT THE HOSPITAL. I TOLD HIM PLAYING THE GUITAR WAS LIKE A DISEASE. HE LAUGHED AND AGREED WITH ME. WHEN I WAS GOING HOME HE SMILED AND SAID" I'M GLAD YOU GOT SICK, COME BACK SOON". I LEFT THE HOSPITAL FEELING PRETTY GOOD, I ENJOYED MY STAY.

A FEW WEEKS AGO I GOT THE IDEA FOR THE COVER OF THIS BOOK SO I TOOK A RIDE TO THE SAM ASH MUSIC STORE IN CARL PLACE, LONG ISLAND I STILL GO TO SAM ASH FOR MY STUFF. I STARTED GOING TO THE BROOKLYN STORE WHEN I WAS VERY YOUNG. MY SON BRIAN CAME WITH ME. I WENT TO THE GUITAR DEPARTMENT WHERE THEY HAD SOME GRETSCH GUITARS HANGING UP, THEY HAD THE NEW VERSION OF THE GREEN OK ON THEM. I ASKED THE PERSON IN CHARGE IF I COULD HOLD THE GREEN CARD WHILE MY SON TOOK A PICTURE OF ME HOLDING IT. HE SAID YES RIGHT AWAY.WHEN HE WAS GETTING THE GUITAR DOWN HE ASKED ME WHY I WANTED JUST THE CARD, SO I TOLD HIM WHO I WAS AND WHAT I WAS DOING. ANOTHER PERSON CAME OVER AND THEY BOTH STARTED ASKING ME QUESTIONS ABOUT THE GRETSCH GUITARS FROM THE 60'S. THEY TOLD ME THEY BOTH HAD THE CHET ATKINS MODELS FROM THE 60' AND HOW GOOD THEY WERE. THEY SAID THEY WERE THE BEST SOUNDING GUITARS

EVER. THEY CONVINCED ME TO TAKE A PICTURE HOLDING THE GUI-
TAR AND THE GREEN OK CARD. THEY WERE VERY CORDIAL TO ME
AND MY SON.

I'M 73 YEARS OLD NOW AND HEARING THEM SAY THOSE GOOD
THINGS ABOUT THE GRETSCH GUITARS PRODUCED IN MY YEARS
AT THE FACTORY MADE ME FEEL GOOD. I TRIED VERY HARD DUR-
ING THOSE YEARS AND NOW THAT I KNOW I DIDN'T FAIL EVERY
THING IS FINE WITH ME.

WHEN MY TIME COMES TO LEAVE THIS EARTH I HOPE SOME-
ONE HANGS THE GREEN CARD ON ME. THE BIG GUY AT THE GATE
OF GUITAR HEAVEN WILL SEE IT AND SAY "LET HIM IN HE'S OK"

HERE IS A PICTURE OF ME AND MY LES PAUL GUITAR IN 1954. WAS I HAPPY ? YOU BETTER BELIEVE IT. I WAS 22 YEARS OLD, I HAD THIS GUITAR, I HAD MY BAND, AND I HAD THIS PLAID JACKET.

THIS IS A PICTURE OF ME AND MY MODEL # 6192
GRETSCH COUNTRY CLUB GUITAR .   I WAS
THIRTY THREE YEARS OLD . IN MY OPINION THIS
WAS THE BEST ALL AROUND PIECE MADE BY
US.NOTICE THE NAME '' DANNY SHAW. '' WHEN I
WAS OFFERED TO PLAY THE HOTEL ROOMS IN
NEW YORK CITY THEY ASKED ME TO CHANGE
MY NAME BECAUSE   MINE DIDN'T SOUND
'''SHOW BIZZ.'' WHEN I WENT BACK TO THE
CLUBS , I TOOK THE NAME WITH ME . I GOT
USED TO IT.

THIS IS A MODEL OF THE GRETSCH BUILDING.
IT LOOKS LIKE THEY HAVE VARIOUS TREES
AND PLANTS SCATTERED AROUND. I DON'T
KNOW WHAT ELSE IS UP THERE BUT WHAT
EVER IT IS I WISH IT WAS THERE IN 1957/1970.
THE SMALL BUILDING ON THE LEFT GROUND
FLOOR WAS THE BANK FRED GRETSCH
WORKED AT ALL DAY EVERY THURSDAY. I
WAS TOLD THAT HE WAS ON THE BOARD OF
DIRECTORS THERE. HE WAS A VERY HARD
WORKING MAN. HE CARRIED TWO LARGE
BRIEFCASES TO AND FROM WORK EVERY
DAY.

THIS IS A PICTURE OF THE OLD
BUILDING BEFORE THE NEW
RENOVATION. DON'T BE FOOLED BY
THE PHOTO, IT WAS VERY WELL
MAINTAINED.

FRONT OF BUILDING ON5/28/05
THIS IS A HUGE DIFFERENCE FROM
THE FACTORY I KNEW. IF IT WAS IN A
DIFFERENT LOCATION AND NO NAME
ON IT , I'D PASS IT BY.

THIS IS THE BACK OF THE BUILDING ON 5/28/05.
ALL THE CONSTRUCTION IS NEW. THE
BALCONIES ARE MUCH BIGGER NOW . THE
THIRD BALCONY FROM THE TOP IS SUPPOSEDLY
THE LAUNCHING SITE OF THE CLARINET ON THE
ROPE.

HERE I AM BACK AFTER 35 YEARS
STANDING IN FRONT OF "REDS"
BAR.ITS TWO BLOCKS FROM THE
GRETCH BUILDING. ALONG SIDE THE
BUILDING IS THE WILLIAMSBURG
BRIDGE. THIS PLACE HOLDS MANY
MEMORIES OF GOOD FRIENDS, AND A
LOT OF GOOD TIMES. IT LOOKS LIKE
THEY'RE GOING TO TEAR IT DOWN.
" RED" PASSED AWAY TWO YEARS
AGO BUT WE'EL MEET UP AGAIN. AS
HE ALWAYS SAID " THAT'S A FACT"

THE MONKEES GUITAR MODEL
WAS A GOOD SELLER. NO ONE
WANTED THE MONKEE NAME
ON THE GUITAR PICKGUARD OR
THE ROD SHIELD COVER.I WISH I
HAD ONE.

Dan Duffy

ALL THE CHET ATKINS GRETSCH GUITARS
WERE BEST SELLERS FOR THE COMPANY
THEY WERE WELL DESIGNED,THEY
PLAYED GREAT, LOOKED GREAT, AND
SOUNDED GREAT. I WISH I HAD
ONE

THIS IS THE SAL SALVADOR MODEL
6199 JAZZ GUITAR . I STUFFED IT
WITH FIBER GLASS TO REDUCE
FEED BACK . I GET THE ITCH JUST
THINKING ABOUT IT.

THIS MODEL # 6135 WAS ONE OF THE
BEST DESIGNED GRETSCH GUITARS.   THE
NECK ADJUSTMENT ROD WAS INSTALLED
THE ENTIRE LENGTH OF THE NECK.   ALL
OTHER MODELS ADJUSTED ONLY FROM
NUT TO THE TWELVE OR FOURTEENTH
FRET. IF THE PLAYER HAD A PROBLEM IT
COULD BE ADJUSTED EASILY. THE OTHER
MODELS   USUALLY   REQUIRED   FRET
REPLACEMENT FROM THE 12 TH FRET TO THE
END OF THE FINGERBOARD.
        THE PLAYER ALSO HAD AN EASY
REACH TO ALL THE FRETS. THIS GUITAR
PLAYED GREAT. I WISH I HAD ONE.

THE "GRETSCH- EN- STINE"
MONSTER BASS WAS BIG AND CLUMSY. ONCE
YOU LEARNED TO HOLD IT YOU HAD THE
FATTEST SOUND ON STAGE, IN THE STUDIO AND
AT THE ADAMS FAMILY REUNION. I WISH I HAD
ONE

THIS MODEL # 6022 FLAT TOP GUITAR HAD
PROBLEMS BACK IN 1957. THE TOP WOULD
SINK IN BETWEEN THE BRIDGE AND THE
SOUND HOLE. A SLIGHT CROWN TO THE TOP
CURED IT. THEY SHOULD CALL IT A CROWN
TOP NOT A FLAT TOP.I DON'T WANT ONE.

THIS IS TRULY A GREAT
CLASSIC GUITAR . I HAVE ONE OF THESE GREAT
INSTRUMENTS. ITS MODEL NUMBER 6001. AT
THIS VERY MOMENT ITS IN THE LIVING ROOM
NEXT TO MY CHAIR.
I PLAY IT EVERY DAY, EVEN IF ITS JUST FOR
FIVE MINUTES. ITS BEEN NEXT TO MY CHAIR
SINCE THE DAY I GOT IT 45 YEARS AGO. THAT
MUST BE SOME KIND OF RECORD.

THIS FOLK GUITAR #6003 FOUND ITS
WAY INTO THE COFFEE HOUSES IN THE
60'S. IT WAS ALSO A GREAT
BEGINNERS GUITAR, DESIGNED FOR
THE SMALL HAND AND EASY FIRST
POSITION PLAYING. USUALLY THE
STUDENT STARTED OUT ON THE
HARMONY "STELLA" GUITAR
(GRETSCH ALSO SOLD THESE) THEN
TO THE MODEL # 6003.

IF YOU HAVE ONE OF THESE JAZZ
GRETSCH ACOUSTIC GUITARS PUT ONE OF
TODAYS " E M G " PICKUPS ON IT.THEY
HAVE ONE THAT YOU CAN HAVE
ATTACHED TO THE PICKGUARD. DON'T
CUT ANY HOLES IN THIS BEAUTIFUL PIECE
OF AMERICAN KNOW HOW, MADE IN GOOD
OLD BROOKLYN,N.Y. I WISH I HAD
ONE.

"Great Chord Changes"
Taught to me by Hy White 1954/1955

Three groups of chords –root on 6th string. Roots on 1-3-5-of a Major chord. G,B,D=G Major Memorize the sequence Major (M), Major 7th(M7), 7TH, 6th. The root note descends the scale Chromatically.

G, F#, F, E, or one fret changing the name of the chord, M,M7, 7th,6th. All chords move up and down the fingerboard. The name of the chord changes according to the root note.

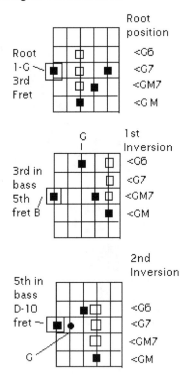

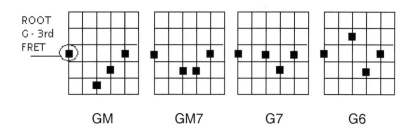

```
ROOT
G - 3rd
FRET
```

GM   GM7   G7   G6

Play this exercise in all keys- Root on 6th string

||: G / / / | GM7 / / / | G7 / / / | G6 / / /   :||

||: F / / / | FM7 / / / | F7 / / / | F6 / / /   :||

||: CM7 | C6 | CM7 |C6   :||

||: BbM7 | Bb6 | AbM7 | Ab6   :||

IMPORTANT – Play these exercises. Memorize them. Make up your own. Play the 4 G chords, then move up one fret to Ab. Play the 4 Ab chords. Move up one fret to A. Continue like this through the 12 keys.

Continued practice with root on 6 string – M- M7- 7- 6 This practice session has you jumping all over the Fingerboard – it will help you finger each chord without hesitation - learn the notes on the 6th string – they are the roots for these chord changes.

CM7	C7	FM7	F7	BbM7	Bb7	EbM7	Eb7
AbM7	Ab7	DbM7	Db7	GbM7	Gb7	DbM7	Db7
EM7	E7	AM7	A7	DM7	D7	GM7	G7
C6	C7	F6	F7	Bb6	Bb7	Eb6	Eb7
Ab6	Ab7	Db6	Db7	Gb6	Gb7	B6	B7
E6	E7	A6	A7	D6	D7	G6	G7

Continued practice with root on 6th string

	C		CM7		C6		C7	
	F		FM7		F6		F7	
	Bb		BbM7		Bb6		Bb7	
	Eb		EbM7		Eb6		Eb7	
	Ab		AbM7		Ab6		Ab7	
	Db		DbM7		Db6		Db7	
	Gb		GbM7		Gb6		Gb7	
	B		BM7		B6		B7	
	E		EM7		E6		E7	
	A		AM7		A7		A7	
	D		DM7		D6		D7	

Play 4 beats to each Chord. Memorize.

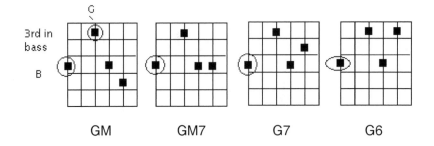

GM   GM7   G7   G6

1st Inversion G Major 3rd (b) in bass on 6th string.

Or you can use the root note (G) on the 4th string.

It's best to understand the 1- 3- 5 – Roots. You should know both.

Play the following studies of the 1st inversion in all keys. Write them down.- This is very important.

||: G | GM7 |G7 |G6   :||

||: GM7 | G6 | GM7 | G6   :||

||: FM7 | F6 | FM7 | F7   :||

||: F6 | F7 | BbM | Bb7   :||

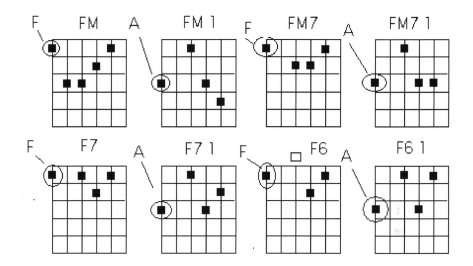

This exercise is on the ROOT position chord and the 1st inversion of the chord, marked with a #1. The exercise written below is on the two Major7. Using the same format do the two Maj7 and 6th.

|BbM7 |BbM7 1 |FM7 |FM7 1 |

|CM7 |CM7 1 |GM7 |GM7 1 |

|F#M7 |F#M7 1 |BM7 |BM7 1 |

|AM7 |AM7 1 |AbM7 |AbM7 1 |

Continued practice on root position and 1st position chords.

Make a copy of page 74. Keep it next to this page for Reference as you practice these exercises if you need it.

Play 4 beats each.

```
|F          |F1      |F7      |F7 1    |

|Bb         |Bb1     |Bb7     |Bb71    |

|Eb1        |Eb7     |Ab      |Ab1     |

|Ab7 1      |Ab7     |Db6     |Db7     |

|GbM7       |Gb7     |B6      |B7      |

|E 1        |E71     |A1      |A       |

|A7 1       |A7      |D7      |D71     |

|G6         |G7 1    |G7      |CM      |
```

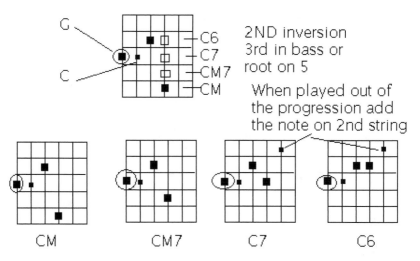

CM   CM7   C7   C6

Finger placement for 2nd inversion – or root on 5th string Optional to play. Remember to learn 1 – 3 – 5 – of scale = a Major chord. Learn in all 12 keys. The 2nd inversion chords will be marked with a 2 after it. On standard sheet music the inversion is not marked the choice is yours.

For example if the music calls for a G chord for 2 or more bars, play the other inversions to add variety to the sound.

PLAY IN ALL KEYS – All 2nd Inversion

|C |CM7 |C7 |C6 |

|Eb |EbM7 |Eb7 |Eb6 |

ICM7   IC6   ICM7   IC6   I

|EbM7 |Eb6 |EbM7 |Eb6 |

Dan Duffy

Continued practice on Root – 1st and 2nd inversions Memorize each
line – do in all keys

|C |CM7 |C7 |C6 ||

|C1 |CM71 |C7 1 |C6 1 ||

|C2 |CM7 2 |C7 2 |C6 2 ||

|C7 |FM 2 |F7 2 |Bb ||

|Bb7 |Eb1 |Eb7 2 |Ab ||

|A7 |D6 2 |D7 2 |G ||

|G7 |Gb7 |F7 |E7 2 ||

|CM7 |C7 |FM7 2 |F6 2 ||

||Bb7 |Eb72 |Ab7 |Db7 2 |

|Gb7 |B7 |E7 2 |A7 |

|D7 2 |G7 |C7 2 |F7 ||

The following chart shows the three inversions of the Major, Major7th, 7th, and 6th. Must be learned in the 12 keys.

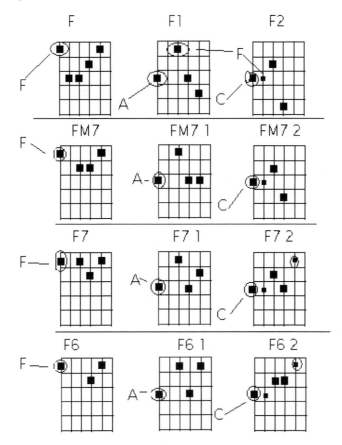

Dan Duffy

MAJOR TO AUGUMENTED – Root position (root on 6 string) 1st and 2nd Inversions. The + sign after the chord name Means (Aug) augmented (raise the 5th note of the chord)

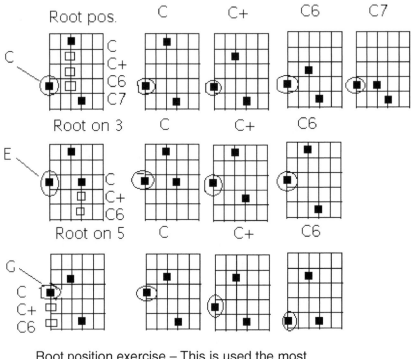

Root position exercise – This is used the most

|C |C+ |C6 |C7 ||

Transfer to all Keys

Minor Progressions – Root position – 1st and 2nd Inversion - Minor to augmented – minor always has a small m as the symbol or min after the chord.

Example: Cm or Cmin - Sometimes C -

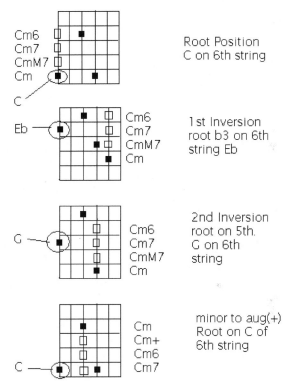

Minor chords – Root on 6th string – 1 in bass

Minor chords - Raise the 5th a half tone or
one fret to change the name of the chord

Root
A
5th
fret
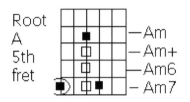
—Am
—Am+
—Am6
— Am7

Fingering for the chords

Am   Am+   Am7   Am6

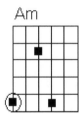 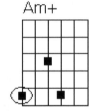 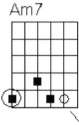 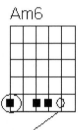

when played out
of progression you
can add these notes

PLAY IN ALL KEYS

|Am |Am+ |Am6 |Am7 |

|Am7 |Am6 |Am+ |Am |

||:Am7 |Am6 (D9) :||

Minor – root on 6th string – Remember – 1-b3-5 of scale = minor chord

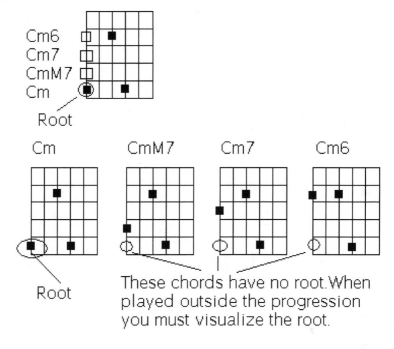

Cm6
Cm7
CmM7
Cm

Root

| Cm | CmM7 | Cm7 | Cm6 |

Root

These chords have no root.When played outside the progression you must visualize the root.

PLAY IN ALL KEYS

|Cm |CmM7 |Cm7 |Cm6 |

|Am |AmM7 |Am7 |Am6 |

Minor continued

1st inversion - Cm - b3 in bass on 6th string

Root on Eb

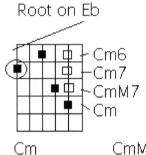

Cm6
Cm7
CmM7
Cm

Cm   CmM7   Cm7   Cm6

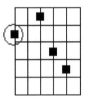 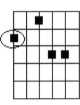 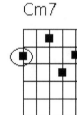 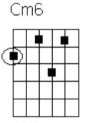

Play in all keys
|Cm |CmM7 |Cm7 |Cm6 |

This is seen a lot
m6 (also called)
m7b5 or half dim

Fm6
Dm7b5   G7

Play in all keys

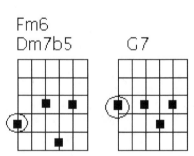

Minor continued - Root 5 of scale - G - on
6th string Opt. Root on 5th string-C-

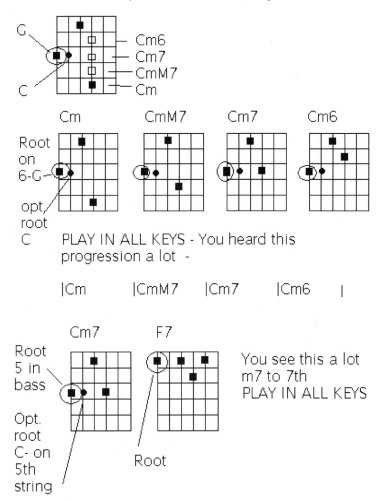

G ⎯⎯⎯⎯⎯ — Cm6
          — Cm7
          — CmM7
C ⎯⎯⎯⎯⎯ — Cm

Cm   CmM7   Cm7   Cm6

Root
on
6-G ⎯

opt
root
C   PLAY IN ALL KEYS - You heard this
         progression a lot -

|Cm |CmM7 |Cm7 |Cm6 |

Cm7   F7

Root
5 in   You see this a lot
bass   m7 to 7th
                                    PLAY IN ALL KEYS
Opt.
root
C- on
5th
string   Root

Minor7th to Dominant 7th - you see
this all the time. You should know at
least THREE ways to play this popular
chord sequence. This is called a 2-5
of a given key. The 2nd scale chord
of a key is a minor and the 5th is the
dom.7th

Below is the fingering for three 2-5
sequence.PLAY IN ALL KEYS-AND
Memorize. Write them down.

Gm7   C7

1
G —

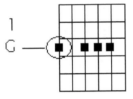 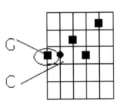

Gm7   C7

b3
Bb —

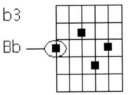 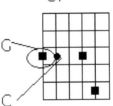

Gm7   C7

5
D —

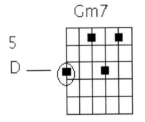 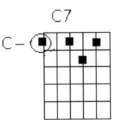

Dominant 9 - b9 - #9 - 13

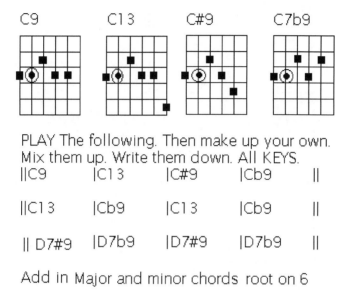

C9   C13   C#9   C7b9

PLAY The following. Then make up your own.
Mix them up. Write them down. All KEYS.
||C9 |C13 |C#9 |Cb9 ||

||C13 |Cb9 |C13 |Cb9 ||

|| D7#9 |D7b9 |D7#9 |D7b9 ||

Add in Major and minor chords root on 6

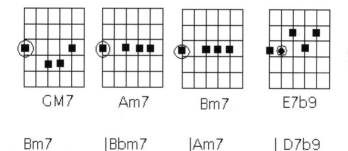

GM7   Am7   Bm7   E7b9

Bm7 |Bbm7 |Am7 | D7b9

PLAY IN ALL KEYS:

Practice on 7th - 9th - 13

Root on 5 on 6

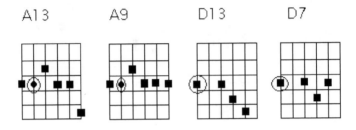

A13	A9	D13	D7

|G13 |G9 |C13 |C13 |

|F13 |F7 |Bb13 |Bb7 |

|Eb13 |Eb7 |Ab13 |Ab7 |

|Db13 |Db7 |F#13 |F#7 |

|B13 |B7 |E13 |E7 |

|A13 |A7 |D13   D7 ||

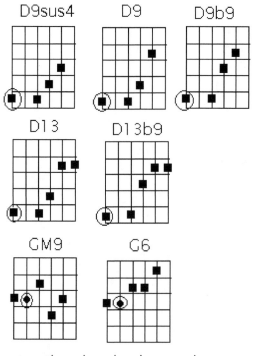

Useing the chords above play
these progressions in all keys

|D9sus4 |D9 |GM9 |G6   :||

|D9 |D9b9 |GM9 |G6   :||

|D13 |D13b9 |Gm9 |G6   :||

|D9sus4 |D13 |Gm9 |G6   :||

DIMINISHED 4 NOTE CHORDS -
HAS 4 NAMES - EACH NOTE IN THE
CHORD COULD BE THE NAME.

Useing the chords below play this
progression in all keys.

Diminished and b9 are
interchangeable

SAME CHORD 4 NAMES

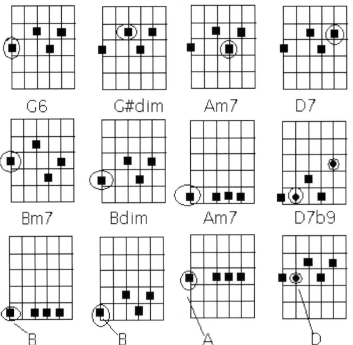

Minor9, 7#9, to 6/9 are good substitute
chords for the 2-5 -1 of key you are in.
They are also used for turnarounds.

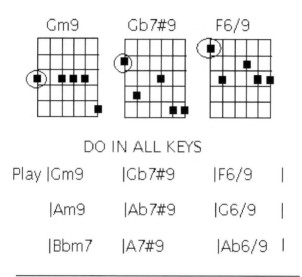

Gm9   Gb7#9   F6/9

DO IN ALL KEYS

Play |Gm9 |Gb7#9 |F6/9 |

    |Am9 |Ab7#9 |G6/9 |

    |Bbm7 |A7#9 |Ab6/9 |

Root on 5-opt. to play

Dm9   Db7#9   C6/9

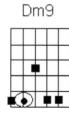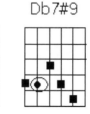

Play in all keys - memorize -
|Dm9 |Db7#9 |C6/9

M7b5 Root Position

Gm7b5   C7

1st inversion

Gm7b5   C7

b3
Bb

G

2 inversion

Gm7b5   C7

G
b5
Db

PRACTICE THE
FOLLOWING
one measure at a time.
Repeat playing it over and
over.
Play each in the 3
inversions.

||:Am7b5 |D7   :||

||:Em7b5 |A7   :||

||:Fm7b5 |Bb7   :||

||:Dm7b5 |G7   :||

||:Bm7b5 |E7   :||

||:G m7b5|C7   :||

||:Cm7b5 |F7   :||

13th, aug7 (aug5) (+5) and b5

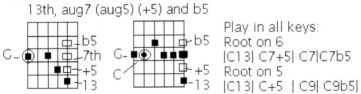

Play in all keys:
Root on 6
|C13| C7+5| C7|C7b5
Root on 5
|C13| C+5 | C9| C9b5|

7b5 chords have one fingering but 2 names
b5 chords are also called #4 or #11

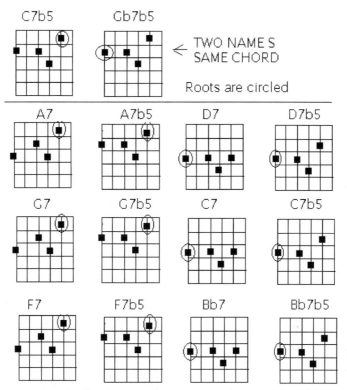

C7b5   Gb7b5

← TWO NAMES
SAME CHORD

Roots are circled

A7   A7b5   D7   D7b5

G7   G7b5   C7   C7b5

F7   F7b5   Bb7   Bb7b5

Useing the fret boxes above to guide you play this
finger twister: A7- A7b5 - D7 - D7b5 - G7 - G7b5 -
C7 - C7b5 - F7 - F7b5 - Bb7 - Bb7b5 - Continue

" TIPS WHEN BUYING A NEW GUITAR "

1)   MAKE SURE THE NECK IS STRAIGHT.
WITH THE HEADPIECE TURNED TOWARDS YOU LOOK
DOWN THE NECK FOCUSING ON THE TOP/RIGHT SIDE
FROM THE FIRST FRET TO THE LAST FRET. AS A RULE I T
IS SLIGHTY CONCAVE.   A SLIGHT ADJUSTMENT IS
NEEDED. ANOTHER WAY IS TO HOLD DOWN THE SIXTH
STRING AT THE FIRST FRET WITH THE INDEX FINGER OF
THE LEFT HAND. NOW PRESS THE STRING DOWN AT THE
14TH FRET WITH THE TIP OF YOUR RIGHT HAND THUMB,
REACH DOWN WITH YOUR RIGHT INDEX FINGER AND
PRESS THE STRING DOWN. IF THERE IS TOO MUCH SPACE
BETWEEN THE STRING AND THE FINGERBOARD THE
NECK NEEDS TO BE ADJUSTED .

2)   MAKE SURE THE FRETS ARE SMOOTH
ON THE SIDES AND NOT STICKING OUT.

3)   MAKE SURE ENDS OF FRETS ARE NOT
POPPING UP.

4)   CHECK THE INTONATION.
MEASURE THE DISTANCE BETWEEN THE NUT AND THE
12TH FRET. LETS SAY IT'S 12 INCHES. NOW MEASURE 12
INCHES FROM THE 12TH FRET TO WHERE THE STRING
SITS ON TOP OF THE BRIDGE.
OR, A TOTAL OF 24 INCHES FROM THE NUT TO THE

BRIDGE. IT HAS TO BE EXACT.

5) IF THE NECK IS CONVEX AND DOES NOT COME DOWN WHEN THE ROD IS LOOSENED A LITTLE (LOOK AT ANOTHER GUITAR.) IF THE ROD IS TOO LOOSE IT WILL RATTLE WHEN YOU PLAY.

HOLD THE BACK OF THE NECK TOWARDS YOU AND TAP THE BACK OF THE NECK LIKE YOU WERE KNOCKING ON A DOOR. IF ITS LOOSE YOU WILL HEAR IT.

6) MAKE SURE THE ACTION AT THE NUT IS CUT LOW FOR EASY 1ST POSITION PLAYING.

7) MAKE SURE THE STRINGS ARE IN THE CENTER OF THE FINGERBOARD AND NOT PULLING TO ONE SIDE BY A TAILPIECE OR FIXED BRIDGE THAT IS ON CROOKED.

8) PLAY THE " FRED GRETSCH BLUES" MAKING SURE THERE ARE NO BUZZING FRETS . PLAY IT ACOUSTICALLY SO YOU CAN REALLY HEAR EACH NOTE . LOUD AMP PLAYING HIDES MANY FLAWS .

9) SET THE ACTION AT THE PLAYING HEIGHT YOU WANT. VERY LOW IS GOING TO BUZZ. THE LOWER THE ACTION THE LIGHTER YOU HAVE TO PICK .

10) THE LIGHTER THE STRINGS THE EASIER IT IS TO PLAY. THE HEAVIER THE STRINGS THE FATTER THE SOUND. SOLID BODY ELECTRIC GUITARS

USUALLY COME WITH GAUGES .009 TO .042. TRY A SET
OF 10'S (.010 TO .046) I PLAY WITH .013 TO . 056. AS FAR
AS STRINGS GO I FIND THAT NICKEL PLATED STEEL
WORKS BEST FOR ME ON MY ELECTRIC'S AND
PHOSPHOR BRONZE ON THE ACOUSTICS, .012 TO .052.
THE ELECTRIC BASS IS USUALLY NICKEL PLATED STEEL
.045 TO .105.
 FOR CLASSIC GUITAR I PREFER A HEAVY 4,5,6.
STRING SILVER PLATED COPPER AND THE 1,2,3RD
STRING CLEAR NYLON. DO NOT USE A MATERIAL
CALLED TYNEX FOR YOUR TREBLE STRINGS. THE
INTONATION IS VERY BAD. A GOOD STRING YOU
SHOULD CHECK OUT IS " ARKAY "MADE ON LONG
ISLAND.REMEMBER I MADE STRINGS FOR EIGHTEEN
YEARS AND FOUND THAT A GOOD SET OF STRINGS CAN
MAKE ALL THE DIFFERENCE.

         11) PICKUPS ARE A MATTER OF
PERSONAL CHOICE. JUST REMEMBER THE CLOSER IT IS
TO THE STRINGS THE LOUDER THE SOUND,
SOMETIMES THIS SETTING MAKES IT HARD TO BALANCE
THE SOUND. THE BASS WILL OVER POWER THE TREBLE
OR DO JUST THE OPPOSITE

         12) FLATOP, CLASSIC AND ARCH TOP JAZZ
GUITARS SOUND BEST WITH SOLID TOPS.

         13) WHEN CHOOSING A FLATTOP OR

CLASSIC ALL THE SAME RULES APPLY. MAKE SURE THE
BRIDGE IS IN THE CORRECT POSITION FOR THE
INTONATION AND IS NOT PULLING OFF, SEE IF A PIECE
OF PAPER WILL SLIP UNDER THE BACK OF IT.
ASK THE SALESMAN TO REMOVE THE PINS IN THE
BRIDGE AND PUT THEM BACK. SOMETIMES AT THE
FACTORY THEY HAMMER THEM IN TOO TIGHT AND
WHEN YOU WANT TO CHANGE THE STRINGS THE TOP OF
THE PIN WILL SNAP OFF.

IN GENERAL ALL THE SALES PEOPLE
WILL HELP YOU WITH ALL YOUR QUESTIONS BUT ITS
ALWAYS GOOD TO KNOW A CERTAIN AMOUNT ABOUT
THE INSTRUMENT YOURSELF.

ANSWERS TO FREQUENTLY ASKED QUESTIONS, FACTS, & MORE STORIES

I would like to start this section of the book with A Tribute to my two best friends who worked with me at the GRETSCH Guitar factory during those years. Fred Rodriguez and Felix Prevette, his nickname was "RED". Fred past away on 12/28/05 and "RED" two years ago. I wish they both were alive to help me with this book. It would have never got done because both of them would be disagreeing on everything. It was all in fun and RED never stopped. After work if we went to the bar to shoot pool, it went on for hours. The loser had to sweep the floor of the whole place while being razzed by everyone in the place. They emptied all the ash trays on the floor as you passed by with the broom. Fred and I swept the most because RED was the best. Red was always gambling and in trouble with the shylocks for paying his tab late. His main thing was PLAYING NUMBERS and SHOOTING POOL.

Red started at the GRETSCH Factory when he was about 20 years old, it must have been around 1948 and he knew all the operations in the construction of the guitars. He started in the woodshop. Vinnie D'Dominico was the foreman at the time and told me a Funny story . He told me that Red was always disappearing during the day and he could never find him. One day he was walking down the center isle of the woodshop and an arm was hanging down from the overhead storage racks for the wood supply. It was RED. He was sound asleep. He always worked part time at night somewhere to help pay his gambling debts. Vinnie got a PIN and stuck him lightly in the hand. Red gave out a scream and a line of curse words and disappeared among the wood in the racks. Vinnie kept calling out "Come down RED, I know it's you."

Red never Answered. Later that day Red was at his bench working and Vinnie went over to him and said . " I know you were sleeping in the overhead racks, show me your Finger." Red put up his MIDDLE FINGER and they both had a good laugh. Red had many places to have a nap, so the game went on.

Red was responsible for bringing the union into the factory. He did a lot to help all the workers get a fair deal from the company. After doing so much for them for five years they voted him out. The company respected him so much for fighting so hard for the workers, that they offered him a position in management. He became the GUITAR ASSEMBLY FOREMAN. Things got a lot better in the assembly department after that . All his experience on both sides of the fence was of great value. He got so upset when the company was sold, he quit. I tried to make him stay and so did Fred but he said," NO." He bought the BAR on South 5th Street along side the Williamsburg Bridge. He had the Business about 5 years and then closed it. He never told me or Fred why.

As the years passed he worked in various places. He eventually found THE JOB OF ALL JOBS as he called it.

He drove the LIMO of a wealthy businessman and woman. He only drove them to dinner and shows, about four hours, three or four times a week and was paid a great salary. They liked him so much they paid all his hospital bills when he started getting the heart attacks. He had the best heart specialist in New York taking care of him. They kept him alive for many years. Finally after four or five attacks he passed away in 2003. He played a BIG PART in making the GRETSCH guitars of the 50's and 60's.

Fred Rodriguez was hired by the factory to work for me inspecting the guitars. He was always on call for Latin record dates. He was a good reader on both Guitar And Bass. We became great friends. Fred loved GRETSCH guitars. Long before Fred worked for the company he bought a 6118 Anniversary Model two tone green when they first came out, and used that guitar the rest of his life. To him that was the best guitar ever made. He had other guitars but according to him they didn't measure up to his 6118. He taught me all the Latin phrases (they are very difficult to read) and I taught him The Hy White chord system. He gave me some Latin record dates when he had two at the same time. A record date was three hours to record six tunes. No rehearsing. There were usually at least ten instruments, a singer and background vocals. I did OK on them and they asked for my card. Once you do a good job, the arranger will call you back. That's how you get in the network. The arranger knows what you can handle.

It was very difficult to get recording dates unless you knew someone. The record dates were controlled by a group of guitar players called THE AMPLIFIER CLUB; they were all good readers and were first on call. I was told they would work around the clock before they would refuse a date, they didn't want any newcomers.

I asked Fred why he wanted the job at GRETSCH and he said his wife was after him to get a day job and just work weekend Gigs. I knew what he meant because I worked a six night a week gig once for six weeks and it almost killed me. Just a few hours of sleep, (if you can sleep) just doesn't make it.

I went to the hospital to see Fred the day before he passed away and it was very sad. He was in and out of a coma. I know he recognized me because he said my name very softly. I believe I'll see them both in the next life and I'll let it go at that.

People always ask me, what's with the VINTAGE GUITAR **SERIAL NUMBERS?** They don't follow in sequence and it's very hard to tell when the guitar was made. First of all we didn't know that you guy's were going to fall in love with these Guitars, collect and put such a high price on them and make them so valuable. If all the guys were still alive they would be as proud as I am for the success of the guitars we made together. I'm also asked what I think of the **Gretsch guitars made in Japan , Korea , China ?**. The true answer will be in fifty years. Will they stand the test of time like the ones I helped make? A lot of you young guys will find out. The serial numbers were kept in rolls in my desk drawer and taken out at random. The girls who polished the guitars were told to use them in sequence. If the main girl was out and a substitute was used for a couple of days to pol-ish the guitars, they went out of sequence. **No one really watched it that**

carefully. The metal plates that were used for the model and serial number were made in advance, and the same thing happened. In 1963 the serial number was stamped on the top of the headpiece, just before it went to the assembly, it was more in sequence control. The numbers continued in sequence following the same order as the labels. The numbers were actually copied from the labels. **In early 1965, [FEB. or MAR.] the serial number was stamped on the back of the headpiece and the serial number system was changed**. The first or first two numbers was the month, the next was the year, and the remaining numbers was the number it was produced in that particular month. We produced around 1500 guitars in one month only twice, and that was in 1964. If you have a serial number with the last four digits over 1500 something went amiss. **The problem with this system is this.** Guitars produced in the months of OCT, NOV. And DEC proposes a problem. If you have a serial number 12632 it could mean that the guitar was made in Jan, 1962 the 632nd guitar made that month. It could also be the 32nd guitar made in Dec. of 1966. The only true way to date a Gretsch Guitar is by the **bill of sale** because most guitars were made on order, they didn't sit in the dealers store too long. Sometimes, if a guitar was made a special color, or anything different from the specs, the serial number came along with the order sheet. **THIS NUMBER WAS PICKED AT RANDOM IN THE OFFICE ON THE 7TH FLOOR AND IS TOTALLY OUT OF SEQUENCE . WHY? I DON'T KNOW.** If a guitar was purchased in 1955 with square hump top position markers, and replaced in 1963 for some reason, it got the new neck with half moon position markers on it. Now you have a 1955 guitar with a 1955 serial number with a 1963 half moon position marker neck and another mystery guitar.

**"The mystery of the HI - LO TRON pickup." WHO MADE IT?
JERRY PERITO. WHO WAS HE?** Jerry was the foreman of the woodshop
where they made the guitar from the beginning up to the point of the final
sanding before the finishing room. You will never read his name anywhere
in any of the books about Gretsch guitars except when I mention his name
as one of the foreman in Bacon & Days book on Gretsch Guitars. Jerry
was always playing around with guitar pickups. He made quite a few different designs that were very good. He always asked me to try them. Every
once in a while as I passed by his desk, I'd notice him making the pickup in
various designs. One day he came to me with the first HI-lo Tron pickup as
we all know it. He asked me to try it, as usual. I was very impressed with
the sound, but it didn't have enough output. He said he could fix that, said
thanks and went back to the Woodshop. He kept improving it until one day
I was called to the showroom. Chet was sitting there playing the first 6119
prototype. They snuck the guitar passed me. I never understood that
. Jimmy Webster was there and Chet was playing it. They both agreed
how good it was. I remember CHET saying "HEY THIS ISN'T BAD". Jerry
Perito wasn't there and no one mentioned his name. It was like the guitar
just appeared there with this new pickup. IT was a secret, no one could
know , no one said "THIS IS A NICE PICKUP JERRY MADE" I didn't
make much of it at the time but 40 years later I still hear guys talk about the
LOVE/HATE HI-LO TRON pickup. Someone on the GRETSCH DISCUS-
SION PAGES (a web site dedicated to Vintage and new Gretsch guitars)
Asked me " What is the history of the HI-LO TRON pickup?" It triggered my
memory back to this GRETSCH MYSTERY. I don't know why Jerry was
never mentioned as the one responsible for the HI-LO TRON pickup. DID
HE GET PAID FOR IT? I don't know , but I doubt it. All the books call it,

THE GRETSCH HI-LO TRON pickup. Why not call it the **JERRY PERITO PICKUP,** after all he made it.

ARTHUR GODFREY'S GRETSCH ELECTRIC TENOR GUITAR turned out to be a very cool experience for me. Arthur Godfrey was a big time television host of the fifties and sixties. He also had a Radio show during the day. REMO PALMIER (A GREAT GUITAR PLAYER) who played in the band for the show came to the factory one day and wanted a tenor guitar for Arthur Godfrey. REMO also told me that he taught Arthur Godfrey the solos he played on his show. I remember they were quite impressive being played on a baritone UKE. I asked him what he had in mind and he told me a FOUR STRING BLACK DUO JET, and would I personally look over the construction of the guitar. We made special 4 pole piece pickup heads and Spacer Bridge. The neck came out perfect and when it was finished Remo came to pick it up. He was overwhelmed with the looks of the guitar. He played a few things on it and I said "Arthur is a lucky guy." . He laughed and thanked me for all I did for him.

The next day Remo called me and told me to listen to the radio show the next day. On my way home the next day I listened to the radio show. Arthur Godfrey said he got a brand new ELECTRIC TENOR GRETSCH GUITAR FROM REMO. He said " I want to personally thank my friend Dan Duffy at the Gretsch Guitar Company for designing this beautiful guitar for me." I thought that was very cool of ARTHUR AND REMO.

I MADE TEN 4 STRING BANJOS VERY HAPPY one day, when I was sent on another mission. It was about 1960 and the singer JIM-

MIE RODGERS had his own TV show. It was very popular. They called the company one day and wanted to borrow the banjos for a SKIT in the show. Naturally they sent me over with the BANJOS. There was a couple of BANJO PLAYERS there who were going to play the banjos off stage, while these **TEN GORGEOUS GIRLS** held the banjos and made like they were playing. The one banjo player (he thought he was my boss) told me to give a banjo to each of the girls. I said "WITH PLEASURE" and proceeded to hand a banjo to each one of these BEAUTIFUL GIRLS. Each one smiled and thanked me as I handed her the banjo. The BANJO BOSS gave me a dirty look. They had a blackboard there with a 4 string fret box drawn on it. They had the dots in the fret box indicating a D7 chord and another box a G Major chord. They wanted the girls to finger each chord to put realism into their playing .Naturally the girls didn't understand so the BANJO BOSS told me to go over to each girl and show her what to do. Again I said "WITH PLEASURE" and I got another dirty look. I spent time with each girl. They were all smiles and giggling. They kept saying "LIKE THIS, DAN?" They knew they were annoying THE BANJO BOSS but they kept it up. One of the girls said "Dan, if you stand behind me and show me where to put my fingers, I'm sure I will get it. Another girl said" ME TOO DAN."

With that the CHOREOGRAPHER said "OK, THAT'S ENOUGH FUN, LETS GET TO WORK." The BANJO BOSS SAID "and we don't need you anymore." I asked the Choreographer if I could stay and she said "NO, BUT THANK YOU FOR EVERYTHING." As I was leaving the girls were calling "GOODBYE DAN." I looked back at THE BANJO BOSS and he was really upset. Two weeks later the 10 Banjos were returned. The PERFUME still lingered ON THE BANJOS, but I left them that way in remembrance of the TEN GORGEOUS GIRLS.

Did **The WHITE FALCON** Guitar receive extra attention when it was being made.? This Is a popular question often asked of me. The guitar went through the same inspection process as every guitar did while being built, no more and no less. When it came to the final inspection, I always had to give it extra time, if it was a stereo guitar. The guitar had many switches, and I had to make sure that they all worked. The Tuning Fork Bridge was always a problem setting the intonation. The space between the pickup bezel , muffler pads, and bridge was very tight. Sometimes the bezel had to be trimmed down because the pickup hole was cut too close to the bridge. The pickup had to be as close to the bridge as possible for the treble response. There were fixtures and gauges made for all the routing cuts for the pickups but I still ran into problems. The Gold binding would sometimes shrink and pull away from the body. A small amount of acetone dropped into the opening, and applied pressure, would solve this problem.

"FRED GRETSCH AND ME." On a rare occasion one day FRED asked me to take a ride with him to a local music store. He heard that the store was doing something he did not like. As a rule he sent Jimmy Webster on such a mission but he was on the road PREACHING THE GRETSCH GOSPEL. I don't ever remember Fred doing something like this before. On the way to the store, FRED told me that he got a phone call from a young guitar player who just bought a COUNTRY GENT. He said He loved the guitar but the store charged him extra for the accessories he thought came with it. He said he paid extra for the Gretsch Guitar strap, The guitar chord, the polishing cloth and the bottle of polish.

When we walked into the store FRED introduced himself and me. The two clerks jumped to attention. One of the clerks said "WHAT CAN I HELP YOU WITH, SIR?" I thought I was back in BOOT CAMP. Remember – This was the height of the guitar boom, **CHET ATKINS, GEORGE HARRISON, THE COUNTRY GENT and THE GRETSCH NAME WAS KING.**

FRED told the clerks what he had heard. They both looked at each other and one of them said "we will have to get back to you sir." Fred said "I'LL WAIT." The answer SHOCKED the two clerks. They thought they could SNUFF him off. WHAT A JOKE, that had no idea who they we dealing with. Fred stood there looking very stern. Just then the owner came out and saved the two clerks. He said "Hello" to Fred and me . They knew each other very well. Fred told him the story and the owner could see he was upset. He made a big mistake when he said "Fred, you shouldn't make such a BIG DEAL out of it." Fred told him "it was a BIG DEAL to the young player who called him with this problem." Fred now went on very calmly and told him that he markets the Guitar and Accessories as a unit, and would he please do the same. The owner apologized over and over again. The store was a **Franchise Dealer** and he could have lost it. He assured Fred that he would make the changes.

The next day Fred came into my testing room and told me that the young player called and thanked him for helping him. He said, the store called him and they refunded the money for the accessories. The store said it was a mistake. Fred thanked me for going with him, put his thumbs in his colorful suspenders, chest out, and went back to business as usual. This indeed was a rare occasion, IT WAS LIKE WE WERE **BUDDIES.**

One day, MRS. GRETSCH was in the office. She came out to the factory looking for her husband. She went over to Fred Rodriguez and asked him if he seen MR. GRETSCH . Fred replied "I'm sorry , but I haven't seen **"THE OLD MAN."** Freddie told me what happened and that MRS GRETSCH got upset when he tried to explain. He told her that in the NAVY the captain of the ship is called THE OLD MAN and is a respectful military expression meaning the leader. Freddie said, she just doesn't like her husband being referred to as THE OLD MAN, and walked away.

Later that day I ran into Mr.Gretsch. I explained what happened and he said He understood. I said many of the employees call him THE OLD MAN or THE HEAD HONCHO and that I call him "THE MAIN MAN." He said "THE MAIN MAN?" I'll settle for that one. He said "Thanks Dan " and walked away smiling.

FRED GRETSCH ALWAYS WORE NAVY BLUE OR BLACK BUSI-NESS SUITS. The 1967 NAMM show was coming up and I believe on the advise of his wife he got a new wardrobe. He didn't attend many of the shows, if he did I think he only stayed one day. He was always the object of friendly jokes by the salesmen and friends at the show because of his suits. They were always cleaned and pressed but they were very outdated. At this particular show he looked real good in his new wardrobe and every-one was telling him so. I never saw him smile so much. He looked like a man who had reached his goal in life. His company out produced and out sold everyone else. He had to be very proud of himself and his company but as far as I know he was very humble about the whole thing. I heard someone say to him. "Fred I don't know which looks best, **YOU OR YOUR GUITARS."**

Everyone knew the name GRETSCH. At the show you always got a name tag with your name and the name of the company you represented on it. As I walked around the show visiting the various booths with their products on display, they saw the name **GRETSCH**, and would always start asking me questions because they all knew the name. In later years when I worked for Vinci Strings and then D'Aquisto Strings the response to the name on my tag was very disappointing. I was so used to the im- mediate attention of the name on my tag that I could never get used to the negative response. They couldn't even pronounce the names correctly. I am not putting down these names, but only a handful of people heard of them.   Although Vinci invented the automatic string winding machine, and D'Aquisto was a famous Jazz guitar maker, didn't make a difference. Jazz guitar represents less than 10% of the whole music industry and is a hard sell. The lack of advertising by Vinci made their product a hard sell also.

I have read on the **GRETSCH DISCUSSION PAGES** website that the famous HUMPED NECK PROBLEM has started to appear on the new line of Gretsch guitars made in the Far East. Well it's nothing new to me, or any manufacturer of guitars. The only difference between them and me is, I did something about it. I described my efforts at GRETSCH, earlier in the book. Importers of guitars don't like to hire guys like me or any other guitar player to re-inspect a guitar when they already paid the factory to do this.

They just want to put a shipping label on the carton and send it out. They soon learn that this does not work. The guitar is a piece of wood that can dry, warp, shrink and crack at any time.

Humped necks are an old issue with guitar companies. They all experience it. Don't believe them if they say **"NOT US"** The main reason for humped necks is the drying of the EBONY OR ROSEWOOD FINGER-BOARD. They dry, shrink , and actually come unglued from the fingerboard and hump up. The same thing causes the end of the fingerboard to push down into the body. The Japanese are very familiar with this problem. **They invented The NECK STRAIGHTING IRON back in the seventies.** It was a heavy iron – shaped like a fingerboard, about 2" thick . It had a temperature gauge and timer. It was placed on top of the fingerboard. The neck was held by clamps that came with it. When I worked for Unicord they imported guitars from Brazil, mostly Classical and steel string acoustics. Every shipment that came in had a couple thousand guitars with humped necks. They had this iron there but for some reason they didn't know how to use it. I tried it and it worked so well that we bought more of them. We made a table that fit about Ten Guitars.

I set up a regular Production System. Ten guitars were set up on the table at a time. The heat was applied for twenty minutes, and cooled for twenty minutes in the irons. They were taken off the irons and another ten guitars were put on. After the iron procedure the fingerboard and frets were redressed, and you had a perfect playing guitar. **WHAT HAPPENS IS THIS.** The heat warms the wood of the fingerboard. The heat loosens the glue between the fingerboard and the neck stock. When the fingerboard cools, the pressure from the clamps glue the fingerboard back to the neck stock **STRAIGHT.** For those who doubt this, I fixed at least fifty thousand guitars with this method. I taught a young guy who worked with me named TOM RIZZI how to use the irons and how to repair guitars in general. He works for another importer now and is doing very well. I'm sure the irons are still burning. He calls me every once in a while to say hello and thank me for all I taught him. I think that's pretty nice of him to remember me. Most people just tap your brain dry and you never hear from them again.

INTONATION - If your guitar goes out of tune as you move up the fingerboard, the intonation is out. First, **CHANGE THE STRINGS. Always have multiple wraps around tuning posts.** If the guitar still will not tune, check the neck. It has to be straight. Sight down the neck on the bass side and glance to the treble. If it has a dip (concave) the rod has to be tightened (clockwise – always loosen strings before adjusting, if the dip in the neck is extreme.) Be careful, you can snap the rod if you over tighten. If you can't see it by eye you can use a straight edge. Place it on top of the fingerboard. Look to see if there is space between the straight edge and the top of the frets. If there is space, tighten the neck adjusting rod. Another way is to hold the 6th string 1st fret down with the left hand 1st finger. With the meaty part of your right hand palm, press down on the 6th string at the end of the fingerboard. With your right hand index finger, press the 6th string down. If there is space between the string and the fingerboard the neck has to be adjusted. A slight space is usually ok. You can check the treble side like this also. **MEASURE THE BRIDGE PLACEMENT** – THE BEST WAY is with a straight edge. Lay the guitar flat, place the straight edge on top of the finger-board – treble side – (1st string) Hold it up against the nut or fret nut. Mark the straight edge at the middle of the 12th fret. It has to be exact. Now hold the straight edge up against the 12th fret and set the bridge on the spot you marked. Measure the bass side the same way. Some players set the bass side a little toward the tailpiece. **Never move the treble side.** Make sure the strings move freely in the nut. If you hear a squeak when you tune the string, the nut slot has to be widened with a small file. You may encounter this, if you go to heavy gauge strings. Check the heel of the neck for a crack. Check for loose braces under the top by tapping the top with your fingers. Make sure all screws are tight on the tuning machines.

If you have a problem hearing the octave at the 12th fret, use one of today's digital tuners.

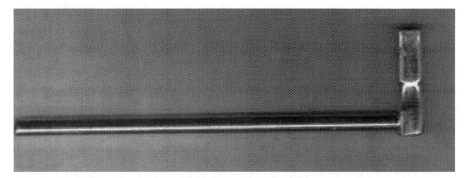

THIS IS A GRETSCH NECK ADJUSTING ROD TOOL MADE IN THE FACTORY IN THE 50'S AND 60'S. IT'S A STEEL ROD WELDED INTO A HOLE OF A GRETSCH DRUM KEY, WITH THE GRIPING WINGS CUT OFF.

"ZERO FRET" - "ACTION FLOW" - We called it the "THE FRET NUT" in the factory. The fret nut was CHETS idea. WE started to use this in 1959. At first I didn't like this innovation, but when I saw the value of it, I changed my mind. I always rejected guitars for a high action at the nut. I always wanted them cut as low as possible to make for easy action in the 1st position. As a teacher, the first thing I did for a beginner student was to lower the action at the nut. A new player has a hard time pressing down the strings, gets disgusted and takes up the **ACCORDIAN**. I don't wish that on any kid, although when **electrified** it has a very cool sound teamed up with GUITAR AND BASS. That was a popular sound in the 50's.

The FRET NUT took the place of the metal nut and worked well. I didn't have to reject the guitars for nut adjustments, the guitars had a better feel, they seemed to play in tune better because the string playing pressure was the same in all positions, it also saved production time **(LESS REJECTS)** When I made the statement about saving production time some of the players on the GRETSCH DISCUSSION PAGES WEBSITE, said that we did this to save money and it's a cheap idea. Production time is very important in the selling price of the guitar. I respect the opinion of every player but I have to say this. From 1959 to 1970 **I NEVER GOT ONE LETTER OR PHONE CALL REJECTING THE "FRET NUT."** Also remember this was Chets idea and he didn't care about cost, he looked at this as an improvement to his guitars.

I have to agree with one player who said   **"ONLY PRACTICE MAKES YOU A GOOD GUITAR PLAYER, NOT THE "FRET NUT."**

THERE ARE NO TWO NECKS THE SAME. Vintage GRETSCH guitar necks were **STRICKLY HAND MADE**. There were no duplicator machines or memory machines controlled by a computer to make each guitar neck the same. We cut off the excess wood from the neck block with a band saw. The neck was shaped with Draw Knives, hand saws, cutting knives, and files. The final shaping was done on a flatbed and spindle sander. Gauges were used throughout the procedure, but we still had to contend with the human factor. Some of the workers were better than others at what they did. The longer they stayed on the job, the better they got. The more we practice the better guitar players we become. It's the same thing. Until the last day, sometime in 1970 when the last guitar was made, it was done this way **"STRICKLY BY HAND"**

PICKUPS - BUTTS FILTERTRON OR DeArmond -

When the company was phasing out De Armond Pickups and replacing them with the Butts system, not everyone was happy. After the change a few letters came in. They said they didn't like the new Butts pickup. I for one, was not convinced that the Butts pickup was better. One day Fred Gretsch asked me how I liked the Butts pickup. I said its good but it doesn't have any **"BALLS."** I said " The DeAmond pickup has more balls." "WHAT?" "WHAT?" Fred kept repeating "WHAT?" I thought maybe he doesn't know what **"BALLS"** means in guitar language. I explained that it means a **"big fat sound."** I told him you have to turn the AMP volume too high, causing a hum, and then the **HUM BUCKING** feature means nothing. Jimmy Webster came to talk to me about my conversation with Fred Gretsch. He said that I wasn't the first one to criticize the Butts pickup. He got together with Ray Butts and improved the pickup. Once I got used to the new pickup, I heard their value in the recording studio. They were clean sounding and they didn't have the hiss like I was frying eggs. This made the recording engineer very happy. The new BUTTS pickup system became a huge success, as we all know. When we first made the change, orders came in for the guitar to have DeArmond pickups. They were installed in bodies with the" INTERNAL BRIDGE BRACING" or "trestle bracing" as they now call it. These guitars have a great sound. I used to switch my fingerboard pickup back and forth from Butts to DeArmond. I could never make up my mind.

There are many Gretsch **MYSTERY GUITARS** as everyone knows. I was never informed about most of them. One day the final TUNE AND ADJUST man, (JIMMY Mc Coy) came to me with the first "7" String Guitar for George Van Eps. He asked me what kind of strings go on it. I told him I would find out and went to see Jimmy Webster and he gave me the strings. He also told me all about George. I told him that I heard the name, but I never heard him play. Jimmy said "you will." The strings were heavy gauge with an .080 for the SEVENTH string. Jimmy Mc Coy and I tried to figure what note the seventh string was. We had a lot of fun that day trying all different notes. Finally we figured it to be a Lower "A".

Mystery Guitars are difficult to remember until someone asks me if I ever saw a particular one. One time I was inspecting guitars coming out of the finishing room. On the rack was six all maple COUNTRY CLUBS. They were BLEACHED WHITE. They were all natural but the whole guitar was as WHITE AS PAPER. They were beautiful and strange. They had none of the brown wood grain of the natural finish guitar. They were assembled with gold hardware. Also on the same rack was some blue sparkle anniversary guitars. These were not the drum cover sparkle colors but real paint. There was red and green sparkle also. They looked like the car finish you see today when you get up close you can see the sparkle.

Jim Mc Coy was The Final Tune and Adjust man (1956 to 1960) in the assembly department. He made the guitar play by leveling the frets and then rounding them off. Setting the bridge, adjusting the nut, and all the rest of the procedures of the final set up before it came to me. Jimmy was a great player and we used to JAM together. He showed me a lot of stuff and I did the same for him. We became great friends. He passed away in 1960 from cancer. It was very sudden. He had it in the stomach and died in the hospital. Like I said before, Fred Gretsch was lucky to have such good people working for him.

WHAT KIND OF GUITARS DO I HAVE? I have my old faithful 6192 COUNTRY CLUB made in 1960. This guitar is like my right arm. It's been all over with me, I would never sell it. My Gretsch "7" string Van Eps IS an outstanding instrument. It's Beautifully made and lots of fun figuring out the possibilities of chord inversions. I made a "7" string SOLID BODY and it has a great sound. I have my GRETSCH Classic. I play it every day because as I mentioned before, it's in the living room next to my chair. I also have a 1948 GIBSON "L7" that my friend Fred Rodriguez gave to me a year before he passed away. I made a pickguard with an EMG JAZZ PICKUP attached, I didn't put any holes in the guitar. I still have my fathers Gibson that went on many adventures with me.

When I was 16 years old I bought a 1935 Buick. It was an 8 cylinder and looked like "AL CAPONES CAR". One night, my friends and I took a ride to a lake about 50 miles away. I always took my Fathers Gibson guitar with me. I'd play and sing in the bars all around the lake. Free Beer And lots of GIRLS. **GUITAR, BEER, GIRLS, A CAR,** what more could a young guy want. We always stayed in the car over night. The next day I was speeding on the back roads when I blew a piston through the block. I left the car off the road and we started to walk. We were only 50 miles from home. Naturally I had to carry my guitar. It took a long time to get home. Was it worth it? YOU BET!

Many times, late at night, I would sneak out of the house with my fathers Gibson guitar, and go to one of the neighborhood bars. I would hang around a while, play the guitar, and sing a few songs. I'd make some lunch money and go home. My favorite place was "KENNELLYS." The place is still there. It has a new name. My son Brian who is a great guitar player told me this story. About 12 years ago he stopped in the same bar on a weekend night with his girl. He said he noticed a guy sitting at the bar that looked like **BRIAN SETZER.** My son asked him if he was SETZER and he said yes. He was in the neighborhood on personal business. My son knew that he was a GRETSCH GUITAR guy and told him all about me, and my job with GRETSCH. He asked about Chet Atkins, and my son told him some stories that I told him about Chet. They talked for hours. My son told him what I was doing now with the string company and went home and brought back some strings. He was very grateful. They had **KARAOKE** that night and they got up and sang some songs together. One of the songs was **"BE BOB A LULA" by GENE VINCENT** My son BRIAN still has the TAPE. **"Kennellys"** Bar has a lot of memories for me and now for the **TWO Brian's.**

Back to the subject of today's **Modern GRETSCH Guitars.**   I met Fred Gretsch after he got the Gretsch name back . I was real happy for him. To this day I don't understand why he couldn't do something with the name before Baldwin bought it. He was now having the Gretsch Guitars made in Japan. He asked me to try them for him. The sound and feel of the guitars did not impress me at that time. The colors and finish of the guitars was very good. I had 7 years experience with Japanese imports at that time working for Univox. I was used to seeing the excellent finish but the sound was far behind American made guitars. When my son took the picture of me holding the 6120 in the music store for the cover of my book, its one of the Japanese guitars made today. At the time I didn't play it. I went back to the store a week ago and played some of the guitars. They are still OK but they all sound the same. They don't seem to have the individual soul that each Vintage GRETSCH Guitar has. If you own a Vintage GRETSCH guitar model 6120 and your friend has the same guitar each one will be different in some way. Even if you don't see it you will either feel the difference or hear a slight difference. I found this in the factory years ago playing one after another. I didn't find this at Unicord playing 50 or a 100 Les Paul copies from Japan.

The music store has a **WHITE FALCON** in one glass case, and a **COUNTRY GENT** in another glass case , the display is quite impressive and reminds me of the old days when the **GRETSCH NAME GOT RESPECT.**

When I worked for Unicord, (now it's KORG) I was told by the buyer for the company, the entire Japanese guitar Bodies were made in one factory and the Necks in another. I know this to be a fact because I opened a case once in a shipment, and the guitar had an "ARIA" logo on the head-piece instead of "UNIVOX." Same guitar, different name. Just a bunch a guitars mass produced, each one without a soul of its own.

I attended the June 2006 Vintage guitar show on Long Island and saw a sacrilege being committed. Famous American GUITAR builders names put on sub par Asian made guitars. They should have the word COPY under the name on the Headpiece. I know this has been going on for quite some time. **I guess they can't make it with their OWN NAME.**   On the other hand, this will make the luthiers **name live on.** I know the guitar is just being copied to make money so I think I'll let the reader decide. **SO WHAT DO YOU THINK?**

The GRETSCH factory always made guitars only on order. When the Guitar boom came, along with the orders, it wasn't unusual to see racks of twenty Country Gents rolling around the factory floor. One hundred 6120's and One hundred 6122's became a common sight.

HOW LONG DID IT TAKE TO BUILD A GUITAR? The guitar took 30 days to complete in the natural production cycle. Naturally we could make one in a week if it was a rush.
I never liked rushing the guitar building process for any order.

HERE'S A CHET STORY, Once when **CHET ATKINS** was in town, he was sitting in the big leather chair, behind the desk in Fred's office. He had his feet up on the desk sitting there like he owned the place. (Maybe he did) He had Fred's letter opener in his hand and was tapping it on the corner of the desk. Chet said he had a great idea for a new feature for his guitars and he wanted me to work on it for him. The idea was to make the guitar sound like a **SITAR**, the Indian instrument the Beatles were fooling around with at one time. Chet picked up the guitar that was in Fred's office. He put the guitar on his lap, picked the strings, and lightly touched the strings with Fred's metal letter opener. The guitar sounded like the SITAR. Chet said, "If you can make a small metal piece come up and touch the strings lightly it will work." He added "just like the muffler." Knowing Chet, he had already tried and couldn't make it work.. I said OK and went back to work. During the next few weeks I tried a few things but they didn't work. The slightest movement of the neck and the crown shape of the bridge made it hard to work on a consistent basis. A few months passed and Chet came to the factory again. He asked me how I made out with his Sitar idea. I told him "GREAT,HERE IT IS" and handed him Fred's letter opener. He laughed and so did I.

FINGERBOARD BLOCK POSITION MARKERS were changed because 1> Chet and Jimmy Webster wanted a whole new look for the Chet Atkins line of guitars. 2 > The factory was having a problem with the inlay work and a lot of filler had to be used. 3> Less weakening of the neck. 4 > As they advertised " The neo classic Feel – Nothing but smooth Ebony."

COMPLAINTS – Difficulty finding your way around the fingerboard on the treble side.

HEADPIECE WINGS – Early Chet Atkins guitars and some other models had what we called headpiece wings, Pieces of wood glued to both sides of the headpiece. They use to crack open where the screws were inserted to hold the tuning machines on . To repair this, the wings were reglued and a piece of veneer was glued over the back of the headpiece, sanded and sprayed black. It looked really good. They started to do this on the NEW guitars until the headpiece was made in one piece.

IF YOUR BRIDGE MOVES - when you use the Bigbsy Vibrato, before you pin it, check to see if the bridge base is flush to the top of the body. If you can slide a piece of paper under the wood base, it has to be sanded to fit. Take the strings and bridge off. Carefully place, and hold a piece of sand paper (grit side up) on the top of the guitar where the bridge goes. Sand the base. The top will give you the right contour to fit the bridge. This should help hold the bridge in place. If the body is too badly warped, sandpaper or two way tape can be used on the bottom ends of the bridge base to hold it in place. Bigsby should have made an adjustable hold down bar, to set the amount of tension on the strings between the Vibrato Tailpiece and the bridge. This would have helped reduce the moving of the bridge when you use the Vibrato arm of the tailpiece.

CROOKED TAILPIECE ? If the bridge of your guitar is moving and causing the strings to come off the side of the fingerboard the tailpiece is on crooked. Hold the body of the guitar and point the headpiece towards the floor. Eye the strings from the tailpiece going over the bridge. You can see the 3rd & 4th strings the best, going over the bridge on an angle. This means the tailpiece is on crooked and has to be moved, or you can shim it. If the tailpiece is on an angle the **body is crooked.** You can see the crooked body better from the back. The proper way to fix it is to sand it straight, but that's a factory job or a repair man who can match the color. If it's a new Modern guitar take it back for exchange.

THE MELITA BRIDGE – Like the FORD COMPANY of the 70's, the GRETSCH Company of the 50's was in the parts business. The Melita Bridge parts. Every day orders came in for the **Thumb Screws, String Rests and Adjusting wheels.** The players were moving the string rests to get the string to tune better. They were taking the bridge apart and losing the pieces. They didn't have a clue about what they were doing.   The directions that came with the bridge said, "Do not move the string inserts." They are preset by the factory. Only move if necessary. If the note is flat move the string rest towards the fingerboard. If the note is sharp move the string rest towards the tailpiece. **REMEMBER** what I said before, IF YOUR GUITAR WILL NOT TUNE - FIRST **"CHANGE THE STRINGS."** I was told, that because of all these problems, they wanted to make a change. They went for the **Spacer Bridge** designed by Jimmy Webster. I don't use a Bigsby tailpiece. I prefer a plain **EBONY OR ROSEWOOD** bridge.

When I first set up my new bridge, I never cut the top of the bridge for the string slots. I space the distance between the strings that I want. I tune the guitar and readjust the spacing of the strings. Then I press down hard on each string with a hard object. Just press hard enough so the string does not move anymore. Each time you tune the guitar the strings get a little more secure. The strings never get caught up in the slots. Natural sustain is improved. You should never cut into the string slots to lower the action (wood or metal) always cut down the base of the bridge. On solid body guitars I like a Stop tailpiece and Tune-o-Matic type bridges. The sustain is naturally better and each string can be set to a fine tuning. I never found a compensating bridge was necessary on my Country Club Guitar.

COLORS – STAINS – PROBLEMS - Unlike other guitar companies Gretsch ventured into the world of color. I was told, the other major companies said GRETSCH WAS CRAZY to go away from tradition and would not be accepted. They were wrong and Jimmy Webster was right. It was his idea. Along with something new always come problems.

When I started at GRETSCH in 1957 the Company was in a transition phase. Some necks had HALF MOON position markers and some had Block inlays, Melita Bridges and Spacer Bridges, All kinds of different combinations were appearing and lots of COLORS. The 1954 Chet Atkins Guitar was advertised as RUDDY/ORANGE BROWN. I remember this darker orange because of guitars returned for repair. I thought this color was really rich looking.

As the years went by they changed to a more RED/ ORANGE. This was advertised as AMBER RED. The Chet Atkins solid body 6121 and 6030 were never big sellers. These guitars started out with the RUDDY/ ORANGE in 1954 and they were made AMBER/RED also.

One time a few 6120 Chet Atkins guitars were returned because the tops faded. They turned a light **washed out** looking orange with no RED at all. In some cases the store owner told us that he had the guitars displayed in his front window. We assumed the sun could have faded them. We always exchanged the guitars. Some players who had the guitar for only six months had the same problem. We refinished them at no charge. The factory had the paint supplier in and changed the clear lacquer formula.

This fading also happened on WHITE FALCONS. They turned YEL-LOW. A certain amount of fading is accepted after time but not only after six months. We stood by our guarantee back then and did the right thing for each guitar and its owner. This always made new friends and sold more guitars. One White Falcon came back twice. **The guitar kept turning PINK.** The second time he sent it back for the same thing, I found a picture of him holding his guitar in the standing position and wearing this bright red band jacket. The problem was solved. I told him the red dye from the jacket was being absorbed by the clear lacquer turning the guitar pink. I REFINISHED THE GUITAR AGAIN. He told me in a letter that he bought a new gold color jacket and takes it off before he plays. He thanked me for solving the mystery. I never heard from him again. About six months later a guy called and said he and his brother were going to buy WHITE FALCONS on the advice from a guy they seen playing in a club. He said his guitar turned pink and I fixed it for him under the guarantee. They asked me if I would pick them out and I said **"OF COURSE"** – and I did.

We experimented with the polyurethane finish in the late 60's because of the HIGH GLOSS it had. I personally didn't like it because it looked like a cheap plastic covering. It was very difficult to work with because it cracked so easy. You couldn't put a screw into it without it cracking. I was satis-fied with the lacquer finish and I really didn't think it was a step forward. I liked the lacquer finish buffed to a high gloss. When Baldwin took over they brought with them a lot of their Burns guitars that had a Polyurethane fin-ish. They had chips and pieces missing all over the guitar. They also had some organs they wanted me to go over. I only checked one guitar. It was beyond reasonable repair. They knew we only did lacquer finishes. I made out red cards and told them to sell at 50% off or junk them. I did the same thing with the organs. They were all busted up. Not worth looking at. They never asked me to do stupid things again.

The Buffers were the hardest working people in the factory. They had to lean hard into the buffing wheel with the guitar. It was very easy to burn thru the lacquer, so it was a skilled job that took some time to learn. They were very proud of each guitar they finished and placed on the rack for inspection. They worked the hardest and complained the least. The dirtiest job in the factory was the Buffers of the metal drum hoops. They got black dust all over themselves buffing metal drum parts before the CHROME PLATING was done.

DUO JETS GET A BAD REP & RAP- when this guitar was first made in the early 50's (1954) Gibson and Fender were already established in the SOLID body guitar market. GRETSCH had a real tough road ahead of them but they never quit. The biggest problem was the reputation of the necks coming off. This was finally solved in 1958 with the screw put in at the heel of the neck and covered with a round disc. It was accepted that way except for the traditionalists,(myself included) The argument for, was Fender had a bolt on neck so WHATS THE BIG DEAL. Gibson was having their problems too. When I met **LES PAUL** I told him I had one of his **GOLD TOPS** with the **TRAPEZE BRIDGE** made around 1950 and he actually flipped out. He said the neck pitch was wrong and the tailpiece was no good and his words were **"GET RID OF IT AND GET THE NEW MODEL"** I told him that I corrected the problems at the Gretsch factory. I told him that I work there and what I do. I said I reversed the strings on the bridge to go over the top of the metal bar rather than underneath and reset the neck and it plays great. He calmed down and said **"THAT'S GOOD, BUT STILL GET A NEW ONE."** I guess he was just embarrassed that these guitars were still out there in the field.

Other players who had Fender guitars told me they were good guitars but only had one good sound. It wasn't versatile, although I heard some players get a pretty nice JAZZ sound on them.

Well, they all had their problems, but Gibson still had the endorse-ment of LES PAUL and Fender had many endorses with hit recordings. The only thing GRETSCH had was a solid body guitar that wasn't exactly solid (it was semi-solid) but it did have a different sound. Along with the unique-ness of being semi solid, a different sound, and all the choice colors, GRETSCH started to hold there own in the solid guitar market. I think the silver jet (the top was drum material) was the most popular of the NITRON top guitars. I remember a GREEN SPARKLE top guitar, black body and neck with gold hardware that was a special order. This really caught your eye. Another special order from a store was for 6 duo jets in the anniversary colors ,TWO TONE SMOKE GREEN with gold hard ware. Red tops, black tops, all the drum sparkle Tops, I believe gave GRETSCH the edge during the guitar boom of the 60's.

THE TRAPEZE Gibson bridge and tailpiece combination on my 1950 Gold Top Les Paul, gave me an idea to have the machine shop make one for me to fit my GRETSCH Country Club. I wanted to see if it would increase the sustain on the guitar. It increased the sustain and I used it like that for years. One day I brought it into the factory to adjust something on the guitar and Jimmy Webster heard the guitar and came to my testing room and asked me "WHATS THAT." I explained what I did and he said "it sounds good" and walked away. A few months later the DREADED TUNING FORK BRIDGE WAS BORN. If only he didn't see THIS BRIDGE, I think we would have been spared the AGONY OF the FLOAT-ING SOUND UNIT

TRESTLE BRACING – SOUND TRANSFER BAR – INTERNAL BRIDGE - ARE ALL THE SAME THING- Different names have come along to describe the Ray Butts – Chet Atkins idea to support the Filter-tron pickups and connect the top of the guitar to the back and eliminate feedback and improve the sustain of the instrument. There is a big differ-ence between the guitars with and without the Trestle Bracing. TRESTLE BRACING gives the guitar more sustain but takes away some of the natu-ral acoustic amplified sound.

The guitars without the bracing have more of the natural guitar sound. Each one is a great guitar. **IT'S YOUR CHOICE.**

Here is the bridge and tailpiece combo I had made and used on MY Country Club Guitar. The hinge was made heavier to hold the angle down to apply pressure to the string bar. It was Gold Plated and looked good in 1960.

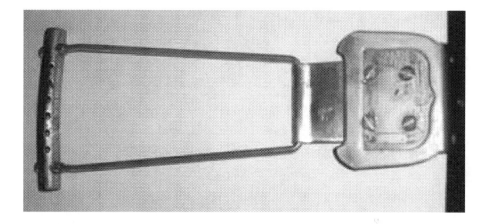

I THINK THIS GAVE "JIMMY WEBSTER" THE IDEA FOR THE TERRIBLE TUNING FORK OR FLOATING SOUND BRIDGE - NO MATTER WHAT YOU CALL IT – IT WAS A CURSE -

The "T" ZONE- Another terrible thing to do to a guitar is, deliberately place the frets wider apart above the 12th fret to get better intonation and play accurately in tune. This does not work. The "T" ZONE was an old "CAMEL" cigarette ad that described the flavor the butt gave you in the mouth and throat and was the exact spot that it gave you CANCER. You didn't get cancer from the GRETSCH "T" ZONE but you sure got a headache trying to get it in tune. THE "T" ZONE and THE TUNING FOLK BRIDGE should be eliminated from all Gretsch history. This should be the last print. ALSO add the TONE TWISTER to the **UNWANTED LIST.**

"IS THAT PICKGUARD ORIGINAL?" "Only if it's cracked!"   The cut outs for the pickups on all pickguards from the 50's were done by hand in the assembly department. The two holes were drilled and reamed for the screws to mount the pickguard. One to the bracket that attaches to the pickguard, and to the side of the body. The other to the top of the guard and mounted to the top of the body at the cut-a-way. These often cracked while putting them on, or a short time after when they were out in the field. When they were made from a mold in the late 50's, or early 60's (I'm not sure when) they cracked even more. Different plastic formulas were tried and after years of rejects and replacements, the cracking got less and less. When a pickguard was replaced it went out from the WHOLESALE MUSIC ACCESSORY department of the GRETSCH Company. They always had a supply of all the pickguards. If you sent in for a 6119 Chet Atkins black pickguard you could get a plain black pickguard or the Chet Atkins signature or you could get the SIGN POST which is the right one. Human error is always a factor.

I heard this many times from the woodshop in my years with GRETSCH, "Don't forget, Dan, there's always the HUMAN ELEMENT involved." This answer use to really get to me. I know that its very true in all business, but if I got 20 guitars at the end of the line with the neck pitch off, sometimes I just couldn't except that answer. So when I don't have the answer to a question, I can only repeat the phrase "DON'T FORGET THE HUMAN ELEMENT." **REMEMBER** if the pickguard is cracked, that's your proof **the guitar is a TRUE VINTAGE GRETSCH.** American car makers recall thousands of their vehicles each year. So why am I complaining?

GROVER TUNING MACHINES were by far the best. The 16 to 1 ratio made it very easy to get a fine tuning on each string. They also held the guitar in tune better than all the rest. They were packed with grease and you can reverse them from right to left. Just open the back plate and do it. One bad thing was the little screw that held the step like end of the machine on. It use to come out and the piece would get lost. We got many complaints and replacement orders. In late 1957 I got the idea of a small LOCK WASHER. I had the machine shop make some and they worked very well. I sent some to the Grover Company with a letter. The next shipment had this little gold plated lock washer on every machine. The problem was solved. The parts replacement business for Grover was over. Do you think they had this little lock washer before I sent them my sample? They never answered my letter, they just installed the **lock washer.**

The Assembly Department had a lot of homemade tools to work with on the guitars. They made SNAKES to install the pickups in the guitars. The snakes were made of thin flexible cable. The one for the input jack had a guitar jack attached to it. You just plugged it in and pulled the wire through. Another cable had a switch cap attached to it. You just screwed it on and pulled the wire through. There was two with switch caps, one for the pickup selector switch and one for the tone switch. A two pronged fork was made to hold and guide the pots to their destination The wooden string winders were works of art. They were hand carved and buffed to a high gloss. Once I had a guy come in and wanted a tour of the factory. He had a camera and I told him **NO CAMERAS ALLOWED.** When I showed him the REPAIR DEPARTMENT he became very interested in Carmines TOOLS. He picked up the string winder and asked me if he could have it. I laughed and showed him the way out. I think the plastic string winder came from this guy.

The Japanese were always coming for tours with their cameras hanging on their necks. There were always 5 or 10 from different factories in
Japan. Fred Gretsch told me "Under no circumstances do they take pictures of the factory operation." Once on such a tour, one of them took out
an ARTISTS PAD and started making sketches. I couldn't believe how fast
and skilled he was. I'm sure he made the GODZILLA movies. I stopped him
and escorted them out. They complained to FRED and he told them very
nicely (without bowing) That's company policy.

It really didn't matter in later years, when we became a SERVICE
COUNTRY, (let them make it, we will buy it , service it, and sell it.) WE
EVENTUALLY WENT TO JAPAN AND SHOWED THEM HOW TO DO IT.
Naturally they say we didn't. Even today I'll bet that when the GRETSCH
Company tells the Japanese to do something a certain way on the guitars,
they say, "It will not work that way." Then they do it and tell you it was their
idea.

"WAS ALL THE WOOD AGED IN 1950 – 1970 ?" To my knowledge,
the company always bought the best woods available. I don't know how
long they were aged for, but the longer they were aged the more you had to
pay. It was like paying rent. Vincent D'Dominco who was very knowledge-
able in this area, suggested at least a three year aging process for the solid
spruce tops AFTER THEY WERE CUT.   Some companies today that supply woods for guitars say they have barn stored wood for 30 to 40 years.
How true it is, no one really knows. A famous JAZZ GUITAR BUILDER,
that I knew for many years, brought me his guitars to try when he finished

them. I think they were the best ever made. They were all works of art. He always respected my opinion even though we disagreed on a lot of things. He brought me a guitar once with a natural finish. I played it and it was really outstanding in every way. I pointed out this little dark brown line in the top near the bridge. He started getting all upset the way he usually did, because he was a total perfectionist about his instruments. He said "the more I sand it the worse it gets." He said his wood supplier charged him a higher price than usual for that piece of close grained spruce just because he gets around $12,000.00 for each guitar. He was in my opinion being screwed. I told him that I think the dark line will eventually crack and he agreed. About 6 months later it did. He was very upset and said "It doesn't matter what you pay, or how long it's dried." **"WOOD IS GONNA DO, WHAT WOOD IS GONNA DO."**

During the guitar boom, it was necessary to set up the wood suppliers to make the sides, laminated tops, back and the neck blanks for us. I understand that Vincent was sent there to set up the operation with all the tools and fixtures. It became an extension of the factory and worked out very well. The factory as big as it was, could not hold the wood that was needed every day. Every day tops, backs and neck blanks came in and went right into production. When they eventually caught up to what we needed, and then some, they stacked them all over the factory floor. I remember one time we made so many guitars, at the end of the month there was no necks, no tops, backs and sides any where in the factory. There wasn't a screw left in the assembly department. Not a single pickup, harness, tailpiece or bridge or tuning machine. Not even one guitar. The racks were empty. I expected a **TUMBLEWEED** to come rolling up the isle like in a **GHOST TOWN** of a western movie. It was very spooky. It was like the storm had come and gone, leaving nothing behind. It was **VERY EERIE.** We all looked around at each other in disbelief at what we just accomplished. When we finally came out of the trance we were in, we all said **"WELL, LET'S DO IT AGAIN."** We kept the pace up until the GUITAR BOOM WAS OVER.

BACK AGAIN TO MODERN GRETSCH GUITARS

The price of the new Gretsch guitars really turns me off. I am not a fan of the copies made in the Asian countries. They are nice guitars made with a good neck fit. The neck has no fingerboard extension and fits flush to the top of the body so that also is a big plus. I had Carmine at the Gretsch factory fit the neck of my Country Club like this in 1960. It improved the sustain and was very comfortable to play with the slightly forward neck pitch. The pickups had to be lowered so the strings didn't touch them. The finish on the copies is also very good. The sound is sub par and the fret work is rough.

I heard one player say "I'M getting a new Gretsch Guitar model # ???" and the first thing I'm going to do is **change the tuning machines, the pickups and wiring harness, and get a REAL BIGSBY tailpiece and bridge.** This does not say a lot for the copies. If all the hardware parts are not as good as the originals, that means the WOOD that the guitar is made of has to be suspect also. This player wants the NAME and QUALITY parts of the original guitar. HE'S PAYING FOR IT WITH THIS OUTRAGEOUS

PRICE so why doesn't he get it? **BEWARE SUITS – IT WONT LAST FOR-EVER!**

  A GREAT GRETSCH GUITAR no one ever mentions was the SHO BRO SPANISH with the spun aluminum resonator. **Shot Jackson** of the Sho Bro company came to the factory in the late 60's. He worked with Vincent De'Dominico in designing and building both the Hawaiian and Spanish Sho Bro guitars with the GRETSCH name on them.

  He had a lot of guitar knowledge and was a great player. He could really handle tools, for such a great player. He and Vincent got along very well. It was really interesting to watch both the guys building these guitars by themselves. If you want to know more about SHOT JACKSON just type his name in the search engine of your computer. You will find it very interesting. I was quickly enthused by the SPANISH model as it had a very unusual sound. I really liked it and had one that I played in my testing room for weeks. I wish I had it now. No one ever talks about these guitars. If anyone reading these pages finds one pick it up and play it. It was designed to have a light (.010) set of strings on it. If you really want to have fun, and if you can put up with some BUZZING, Try 9's.

  My GRETSCH COUNTRY CLUB and me seen a lot of action around the Brooklyn and Queens area playing in all the clubs. One Saturday night in a club in Brooklyn three guys and one girl came in the club and sat in a table near the band stand. I knew right away they were part of the local boys that owned this part of town. This was the first of many nights they came in the club. They usually came in about two in the morning and were still there when I left about Three AM. One night they asked me to join them at their table when they came in. They told me how much they like the way I play. They requested some songs and I played them when I went back on the band stand. When it was Three AM and time to quit they asked me if I would stay and play some tunes for them. Of course I said "YES". I stayed and played for them till about Five or Six o'clock in the morning. We became very friendly and they came in every Saturday night and I always stayed late and played for them. It was always a party atmosphere. They always drank SCOTH AND CHAMPAGNE CHASERS. The owner of the club never said a word, he just kept serving them. They always made it worth while for me to stay and play for them. One night as they stuffed some cash in my pocket I said "Thanks, but that's not necessary." They gave me a look like I insulted their mothers, and I quickly said I was sorry and didn't mean to down grade their enormous generosity and that I just felt guilty about the amount of money they gave me. Their death looks turned into (NOT SO OFTEN) smiles and they said "Dan" , "YOU'RE A STAND UP GUY" "and we like you." After that I just went along with the party. They were actually some of the best guy's I ever met. They reminded me of my friends I grew up with when I was very young in the streets of Brooklyn and Queens. You could trust them and they could trust you, not like some of the people I met it the Music Manufacturing business.

One Friday night in the club, after I finished playing a set, I was standing next to the bandstand talking to a girl I knew. The next thing I remember is waking up underneath some tables laying on top of my guitar. I had an enormous pain in my head. The guy's in the band tried to pick me up but I said for them to wait because I couldn't see. Eventually my vision came back but was very blurry. They told me a big gorilla hit me in back of the head. They said he was drunk and just went wild. I went home and the next day I went to the doctor for the pain. He said I had a concussion and I should stay in bed for a few day's and rest. I took the pills for the pain but they didn't help much. I stayed in bed for a few days. I went back to work after a day or so. Both my eyes were BLACK AND BLUE from being hit so hard in the back of the head. I was embarrassed walking into the GRETSCH building so I wore Sun glasses. Jimmy Webster was the first to spot my two black eyes and said "That's why I quit playing nights, its safer here". I agreed.

The following Friday night I went to the club. It was my last two nights of a six week contract. My eyes were getting better but were still a little black. Every one was checking out how I looked. After the second set this BIG GORRILLA comes up to the band stand and say's "I'm sorry for what I did" I told him he almost killed me and let it go. The next night the three guy's and the girl came in. After the set I went over to them and said hello. They said they heard what happened and wanted to know if the BIG GOR-RILA APOLOGIZED to me. I said that he did. They said he'll never bother you or anyone else again. I thanked them and let it go. I said goodbye to them later that night, and told them it was my last night, and that I will be in a club in Queens for six weeks, if they want to see me. They said "WE'LL BE THERE DAN" and I grabbed my guitar and amp and left. They never came to the club in Queens. After about a year I went back for another six weeks in that club and I never saw the BIG GORRILA or the THREE GUY'S AND THE GIRL. It was like they never existed. I still think about them today after all these years.

Another time, I finished a gig early and I stopped in a local bar before I went home. The owner was a friend of mine for a long time so I stopped in to see him every once in a while, it was about two in the morning as I sat at the bar talking to this guy I knew from the neighborhood. We were the only people there. I had my Country Club Guitar in its Grey plush lined case leaning against the bar next to me. I heard the door to the bar open behind me. I looked at my friend behind the bar and he was looking at me with a strange look on his face. Suddenly I felt something cold push against my neck. **IT WAS A GUN.**   Suddenly another guy was standing next to my friend behind the bar with a gun to his head. He came in the back entrance. The guy leaned over and patted me down to see if I had a gun. He said "we want nothing from you, all we want is the bank" The **"BANK" is the money taken in all day and put in a small metal box and hidden somewhere in the bar.**   Only a small amount of cash is left in the cash register at a time. Just enough to make change.   **REMEMBER,** if you ever pull a stickup, ask for the bank. The robber told me and the guy next to me, to get up , don't turn around, and go into the MEN'S ROOM. I got up, grabbed the handle of my guitar case and started to walk to the men's room. He pushed the gun into the back of my head as he escorted us there. He didn't say anything about my cherished guitar that I held onto very tightly.

While we were in the men's room I could hear them threatening my friend, the owner. I knew he would give them the bank because he wasn't stupid and there wasn't that much money in the box anyway. There never was. The guy in the men's room with me was starting to panic and was trying to rip the bars off the window trying to get out. The metal bars were to prevent guy's from breaking in (WHAT A JOKE).   I told him to be quiet or they would fill us full of holes and flush us down the toilet. I wrapped my money in a paper towel and hid it in the bottom of the waste basket. I probably had more money on me, than was in the bar's bank. I didn't want to take a chance in case they changed their minds and wanted our cash too. I left a few bucks in my pocket just to keep them happy if they did.

After a while it was very quiet, so I went out. The other guy started to pull on the bars again as I left the men's room. I called out the owners name but he didn't answer. I found him tied and gagged, in the kitchen, in the back. He was still shaking as he called the police. The police took two hours to get there. When they finally got there they went through the usual questions, paper work and were gone. The next afternoon while I was teaching , I remembered the gig money I hid in the trash basket in the men's room. When I was done teaching I went straight to the bar. I thought it would still be there because the men's room never got cleaned until someone complained. When I got there I went straight to the men's room and the waste basket. The money was still there just like I left it. I put it in my money clip and went out to the bar. My friend came over and said "THEY GOT THE BANK." All I thought was **I STILL HAVE MY COUNTRY CLUB GUITAR.** Believe it or not that's the only thing I was thinking about through the whole thing.

Another time I was on the band stand in a club on Long Island when a guy came in Yelling "WHERES MY WIFE" over and over again. When I looked at him I saw he had an **axe** and was waving it around as he was yelling. All the people were screaming as he came up to me. I forget what I was playing but I remember protecting myself with my guitar. As I held my guitar in front of me and stopped playing he shouted at me "WHERES MY WIFE?" I said I think she's in the lady's room, just to get him away from me and my guitar. As he went in there, the cops came in. I told them he's in the ladies room. They started to shout for him to come out. I heard a lot of screaming and chopping coming from the ladies room. When the cops finally got the door opened, without breaking it down, they found a large hole in the wall and he was gone. **HE CHOPPED HIS WAY OUT.**

"The rise and fall of a Guitar String company"

GUITAR STRINGS – I spent about 20 years in the manufacture of **GUITAR AND BASS STRINGS.** I started with **"VINCI"** Guitar Strings about 1978 as General Manager. I didn't know that I was General Manager of nothing. I first met TOM VINCI when I worked for Unicord. The company bought Vinci strings to replace the strings on the guitars that came from Japan and Brazil. The guitars were equipped with bad strings and they still are in my opinion. Tom's father invented the automatic string winding machine around 1952. He also made his version of the automatic ball end machine. The BALLEND machine put the brass ball end on the round wire for the Plain Strings and the HEX CORE WIRE for the Wrapped strings. The BALLENDER was capable of making 15,000 plain strings in an eight hour day. Almost Every Guitar String Manufacturing Company has a couple of these String Winding Machines made by Vinci. They always had to buy two machines because they knew they could copy the machines in their own machine shops. I think the only U.S.pattern Vinci could get was - "no one could copy the machine and sell it – but they could copy it and use it"

The first time I visited the Vinci factory, I was still working for Unicord. They had a large factory which they owned, and the factory next door that they owned also and rented. I didn't know the father owned everything and he always reminded Tom that he did. I thought he really had a great setup with about twenty four machines and two Ball End Machines. One made plain round strings, and the other made the hex core wire.

I said in the beginning, I didn't know I was going to be General Manager of nothing, because when I went there the first day there was nothing there. He had a **FIRE**. All the machines were gone except for a couple that were being refurbished to be sold. So here I was again, starting from the ground up in a business I knew nothing about. Having all the past experience and knowledge of the guitar really helped. He had a few orders there but it was just about over for the company. The only calls that came in were from suppliers who wanted their money. There was 4 girls there packaging strings. The strings are coiled by hand one at a time and put into a 4x4 envelope. One gross of each gauge of the string set was prepared like this. When the six gauges were finished, they were collated into 144 sets (1 GROSS) with a cover on each, and put into a 4x4 plastic pouch. Then into a small box that held 12 sets. Then the 12 doz. Boxes were put into a special made carton that held them. One carton held 144 or 1 gross sets. GOT IT? All production was done by the gross. After a while and a little convincing we decided to start up again. We started buying bulk strings from the manufacturers and packaging them with the Vinci name on them. Tom knew all the string makers because of the machines him and his father made and sold to them. There was no money, so every thing was done on

30 days terms. They were lucky if we paid them in 90 or 120 days. They all knew Tom's father was wealthy AND HIS CREDIT WAS IMPECCABLE. Not that he was going to help Tom, but they didn't know that. It took a lot of work and begging from Tom to get help from his father. We went along buying and selling strings but not getting anywhere because of all the money he owed.

The first winter came and the factory was in bad shape. There was leaks everywhere. All the pipes were frozen in the bathrooms. There was ice everywhere. The floors were frozen and slippery. There was no money for oil to heat the building. We had to heat this enormous building for just seven people. This didn't make any sense. I got the idea to move the four girls and the whole packaging operation into the front of the building. There was a very large conference room next to the office that Tom and I used. The accounting firm for the company was there twice a week checking the books to see if any money came in so he could grab some. The company owed them a lot. They also charged (I think) $200.00 a day every time they were there, so we were getting no where with their bill. **I SEALED ALL THE DRAFTS IN THE CONFERENCE ROOM.** I got six space heaters and set them up. The place got warm as toast and we were able to get through the winter.

There were a lot of strings in the factory that were discolored by the fire he had. They were mostly acoustic 80/20 brass and phos.bronze. I looked them over and took an inventory. If we sold them at a low cost we could make $250,000.00. This would solve a lot of problems and send us on our way. Tom said he knew a cleaning solution that might work. We got the solution and I started cleaning the strings. They were tied together by the gross. You had to untie the gross and put the strings in the solution. Then you had to move them around for a few minutes and take them out. Then you rinsed them off with water, tied them back together in 1 gross and hung them all around the factory to dry. You had to wear rubber gloves, old shoes and clothing because it was an acid based cleaning agent. They turned out so good that some were brighter than new. We started shipping them out on orders and things started to slowly change.

The machine shop that Tom's father owned was in Brooklyn. He was still making the machines there. He said he hired a machinist who was very good and he could put together a couple of STRING WINDING MACHINES for us. His name is ANTONIO and we would work together for the next 20 years.

Antonio made four machines. Two for Classic strings and two for steel strings. We started making the strings in the machine shop and Tom would bring them out to us on Long Island to fill the orders.

Vinci had a chance to rent the big factory we were in so we moved to a place his friend owned. It was rent free. It was in the basement of a large factory on Long Island. There was water dripping everywhere into puddles on the floor. I had to keep everything on skids . I tried to keep everything dry and away from the water. There was gnats everywhere and once again I thought I was back on PARRIS ISLAND being eaten alive by those things. The girls found a spray that kept the gnats at a distance. Every day, I thought of walking away from this insanity but I always felt the potential was there for a good future. Finally after lots of gnat bites and wet feet we found a small store to do the Packaging in. The only down side of this place was all the supplies were in the basement. There was a lot of up and down stairs.

We had heavy duty racks to hold about 250,000 4x4 envelopes. The envelopes came in small boxes. Each box held 1000 envelopes. I had to continually haul envelopes to and from the printer. There was always an argument about when he would be paid. He also printed the covers for the string sets. We needed our own printing press. You need a lot of printing done in the string business. Six envelopes and a four color cover for each set. Half the cost for a set of guitar strings is the packaging. The sets that come with the six different colored ball ends to determine the gauge of the string, is called environmental packaging. No envelopes, no cover, no plastic pouch just a printed plastic sealed bag. You still have to coil the strings by hand, but it costs less for material.

We went on like this for a while, slowly building up the business. We had to do a lot of private label business.

Private label is supplying anyone with their name on the package. Many of the Guitar and Bass string sets hanging in your favorite Music store is private label. All the Major String Makers do this. You really don't know who made the set of strings unless it said so. Private Label was a big business and I guess it still is.

When we first set up the little store, Antonio came out with Tom from

Brooklyn. He helped me set up the racks in the basement. He was from Argentina but he was already speaking some English. He was determined to become an American citizen, and with a lot of hard work and studying he did. He said this was a dream come true. Eventually he spoke like he came from Brooklyn, just like me. Maybe **"DATS"** not so good. We got together and worked like a team. I always took care of the books. I paid the bills and made up the payroll. This was always a struggle. There never seemed to be enough money. The more business we did the more supplies and people we needed.

One day Tom came into the store with Antonio and said he wanted to show us something. We drove to the old factory that we started in. Right across the street there was another smaller building on the corner. He said "come on," and we followed him. He stopped in front of the building and said **"WE JUST BOUGHT THIS BUILDING."** I was speechless and I could see Antonio felt the same. I wondered if this was the reason I had so much trouble paying the bills.

Tom came to terms to pay off the accountants. I guess I wasn't such a good bookkeeper. After we moved into the new building his wife took care of the books like she did when they were close to bankruptcy,(that's my opinion,) but just didn't file.

Antonio and a couple of men we hired, started to prepare the building for the machines. They had to run lines for the air compressor, needed to operate some of the functions of the machines. They built a wall out of cinder block to make a separate room for the machines. I don't think there wasn't anything Antonio couldn't do. When the factory was ready the moving started again. It seems that all we did was move around but this time it was different. This was our own building. We came a long way from the freezing cold building across the street. Moving those machines was always a hard job. One time one slipped and it pinned me and Antonio against the wall inside a truck. I really hurt an already very bad back and **Antonio's thumb was hanging off.** I took him to an emergency room and they sewed it back together.

Antonio started to build more **WINDING MACHINES and BALLEN-DERS.** The machines were getting better and better. Antonio was changing a lot of things from the original design. I think he made 26 String Winders and 3 Ball End machines. We also got our own printing press to do the envelopes. This machine ran all day. When a part broke Antonio made a new one better than the old. He made the printing press work better than new. The press had metal plates with the gauges on them that I had made the Art Work for. Later we used some form of hard rubber. When they wore out, I got replacements Other plates had our LOGO on them also either Acoustic or Electric and what ever else was needed to describe the contents of the 4x4 envelope.

Making guitar and bass strings is a lot easier than making Guitars. Working with wire is a lot easier than wood.

The wire companies supply all the string makers, so they know exactly what you need. There is no mystery to it. The only problem you have with wire is the tarnishing. Also, the wrap wire has to maintain a special strength so it does not spring back after it is wound on the core wire. If it springs back just a little the string will have a dead sound. The tension of the wrap wire has to be tight. The wire passes thru this tensioning device and is held at a certain tension during the wrapping process. Antonio devised a tensioning device that was controlled by a small computer. I used to randomly put the strings on my guitars at home or in my office to keep checking the quality. We tried different formula of wrap wire and core wire to come up with a good sounding string. **Jerry Garcia, Neal Shawn and Tony Rice** were some of our endorses. They really loved the strings.

When we settled in the new building, I started doing a lot more sales by hiring salesmen for the different parts of the country. Eighty percent of our business was in Europe. The salesman already had their accounts so it was easier than I thought. They represented (Rep for short) a lot of companies so all the stores knew them. I set up a program for them with the percentage they got. They liked the whole program and I treated them very fair. They got all the samples they needed, to leave with their customers to try, and the orders started to come in. Everything started to come together. Every small order that went to the stores in the States went out COD. I was managing the Payroll with just the COD orders. I had this plan for a long time, but it took years to achieve. It worked for a while but then sticky fingers got in the way. The old way was starting to appear. It seems some people never learn. They disregard all the people around them and only think of themselves. They forget what these people have done for them and destroy it all with their greed. After coming back all that way, you'd think they wouldn't repeat the same stupid greedy nonsense. We were doing over two million dollars in sales a year. Every one was making a decent salary. In the beginning a lot of us had to go weeks without a paycheck. Why this happened - I don't want to get into. When I worked for Unicord an incident happened that made me think to myself **("this GIG will be over soon")**

A very hard working guy from the office stopped by my desk every morning. He never took a day off. He was the first one in and the last one to leave. One day as he stood talking to me, two guys walked up behind him and put him in **handcuffs.** They were Detectives and they arrested him. He just looked at me and said "I'm sorry Dan." He embezzled $250,000.00 that they knew of. I never heard of him again. I think this was one of the reasons the owners of the company CLEANED HOUSE. It seems that no matter where you work, these people are around, lurking in the shadows acting like nice guys ready to do their thing.

Back to my story - After phone calls came in threatening to blow up the building I knew we owed more than just wire bills. I couldn't believe what was happening. It didn't take long for the company to get so far back in debt that the whole thing got to me and I walked out. As I drove home I was thinking of what I did. All the business we worked so hard to get. All the machines ANTONIO built. Every one who seen the business we built was amazed. I left everything behind. I was sixty now and I still had to work. All the machine operators would be out of work also. Everyone who stayed with the company from the beginning was on there way out and there was nothing I could do. **NOT THIS TIME.**

Two months after I walked out, ANTONIO followed me. After we walked out we were accused of stealing everything in sight. About six months later after we were gone, a private investigator made a video of the culprit loading the company station wagon with the packaged inventory to sell it cheap in the city for cash. This was indeed greed and insanity combined. This was destroying everything that everyone worked so hard to achieve. I don't know the exact ending of this story. I understand everything was sold in order to pay all the debts. This story is not intended to harm the Vinci name. It's a story of what can happen to anyone, anytime in the music business. I helped create the Vinci guitar string and its quality name in guitar strings. I hope it continues to make the great strings, like it did years ago. It probably does. I'm sure they have the same great machines that Antonio built and are putting them to good use. As long as they are hard working people in charge, they can't fail.

When Antonio left he went to the Mapes piano string wire company to work. We bought some of our wire from them. They are a very old company that supplies core and wrap wire to the whole industry. They also make strings under their name MAPES. Years earlier, they bought an old ball end machine they couldn't get to work so Antonio fixed it for them. They visited our factory many times. They knew his skills and hired him on a phone call. After one day there he called me and said he was coming back from Tennessee and wanted to talk to me about starting our own guitar string company.

We rented a small unit in an industrial area. We went out and bought a Lathe, milling machine, drill press, industrial saw and what ever else we needed to make a small machine shop. Antonio knew exactly what we needed. He set up the lathe for me to operate. I drilled miles and miles of holes through round aluminum pipe. Every part of the machine was inside Antonio's head. He made notes on how many pieces of round or square parts was needed. My wrist was in a lot of pain from turning the lathe. I tried all kinds of different things wrapped around it, but nothing helped. When I was almost finished drilling the miles of holes, Antonio fixed the lathe to run automatic. The joke was on me. Antonio was a wizard on the Milling machine. He made every single part, small or large on this machine. He also knew how to set up the electronics for the machine. I think he is the GEORGE VAN EPPS of the Guitar string and machine making business. Just like George plays the "7" String Guitar [Knowledge, Creative, and Precise] Antonio makes Guitar Strings and Machines Needed for the guitar players needs.

We made four **GUITAR STRING WINDING MACHINES.** Two would be for us and two we were going to sell to Jim D'Aquisto and his partner who would put up the money. We were going to financially support our company by building machines for them. It was hard to get guitar string orders from the people I knew because of the lies that were told about us when we left Vinci. I knew that some day the truth would come out but it was taking too long. Antonio and I decided to go in partnership with them for a small percentage of the business. We put up our small machine shop and our two winding machines. Jim D'Aquisto put up his name and his partner put up the money. They knew nothing about making or selling strings. Jim had a small string business buying strings and putting his name on the label. I made and packaged his strings for him when I was with Vinci. Jim was prompted to do this because Vinci was sinking fast because of sudden lack of funds. Jim was supposed to just put up his name, stay home, make his guitars and stay away from the every day business of the string company. This did not go well with him. After about a year his name wasn't living up to expectations and the business was doing practically nothing. From the beginning the DADDY BIG BUCKS did not want to make private label strings. This was a big mistake and I told him so.

Jim and Daddy Big Bucks were at each others throats constantly. They weren't coming around much any more so I decided with Antonio to do it my way. The way that was successful at Vinci for so many years before the Greed took over. DADDY BIG BUCKS approached me about the same time and said he wasn't putting in any more money and that Antonio and I have to take a cut in salary. After speaking to Antonio we did. He wasn't happy about this saying "THAT WAS PART OF THE DEAL," "LOOK AT THESE MACHINES I BUILT, and Look at the sales your getting he's reneging on everything." "Jimmy's name don't work and now he doesn't want to pay us, lets take our machines and get away from these two guy's." I told him it wasn't that easy and that the company owned everything we did. We were trapped. I kept a record of the amount of money we were owed and later when the sales were coming in I told DADDY BIG BUCKS we were going to start taking back the money we were owed. He wasn't happy. He thought he beat us out of it. Right after that, the money man came and told me he was going to court to be sentenced. I didn't know what he was talking about. He explained to me that he was convicted of **BRIBERY. He told me he bribed buyers for government contracts** in his other business and was caught. Antonio and I were really off the wall. If we had a lawyer at the time we probably could have done something. He should have told us this before we went into business together. I know I would have stayed far away him. He was sentenced to six months home lockup with the bracelet on his ankle to monitor his whereabouts.

I set up a whole Private Label and Bulk String Program for EUROPE and the business started to come in. Salesman for our stores in the various states in the U.S. were given a Private Label Program. They were also given a monthly sales discount promotion on certain D'Aquisto Label sets. The company was now in first gear and moving. It took about four years after that to hit close to a MILLION DOLLARS IN SALES.

Once again GREED lifted its ugly head. It was no surprise. I seen it many times before. Jim D'Aquisto passed away after losing his name in a court decision. I retired and Antonio left soon after to open his own Company with his Son. We left behind 26 String Winding machines and Two guitar ball end machines. We did the same thing for the second time. The approximate sale value at the time, for all the string winding equip- ment was about **TWO AND A HALF MILLION DOLLARS.** You definitely need your own Lawyer when you go partners in business. You can't trust anyone. When someone wants to make a deal with just a handshake you better run. The old joke about counting your fingers after a hand shake is very true. These guys are nothing new, they just think they are. In the end they either go to jail or live the rest of their life in misery **BECAUSE THEY ARE MISERABLE TO BEGIN WITH.**

I knew Jim when he worked for John D'Angelico in the late fifties and sixties. D'Angelico made great arch top guitars and Jimmy wound up making better guitars than his teacher. Jim was not a healthy guy when we were partners in the string business. Sometimes he would call me every curse word he could think of. This was not the guy I remembered, when I was making his strings at Vinci. Although we had our bad moments, we

had some laughs. Once we had to go to the NAMM show in California.
The day we were leaving we had an ICE STORM and we missed our flight.
When we finally arrived at the airport, we went straight to the assigned
boarding area. There was no one there except the girl behind the counter.
We went up to her and presented our tickets and boarding passes. She
said **"YOU MISSED YOUR FLIGHT SO I'LL HAVE TO GET YOU ON
ANOTHER ONE, STAND OVER THERE AGAINST THE WALL AND
WAIT."** Jim went **WACkO**. He said "are you A **NUN?"** "Are you Sister
Mary Margaret that I had in Catholic Grammar School?" **"DO I LOOK SIX
YEARS OLD?"** Do I have little blue shorts on and my little blue tie?" "Who
are you to tell me **TO STAND AGAINST THE WALL?"** He kept it up until a
guard came over and told us to quiet down. Jim asked the guard if he went
to Catholic school and he said yes. Jim said "that girl thinks she's a **NUN"**,
she told me to stand against the wall and wait." The guard looked at
me strangely, and said "Sir, please cooperate." I finally calmed Jim down
which was next to impossible. We were assigned to another flight and
boarding gate. Jim and I walked there laughing.

When we were at the NAMM SHOW in Frankfurt, Germany, we had a
nice twenty foot display booth with all large simulated pictures of the packs
of strings. It really looked good. No one knew the name D'Aquisto except
for a few Jazz people who were familiar with the GUITAR. It was quite em-
barrassing. I had to repeat the story behind the name all day long. They
couldn't even pronounce it. Diaqueve, duiqueti, dayqeesti, I heard enough
different ways to pronounce the name than I thought possible. I thought if
they couldn't pronounce it, how could they remember it to place an order.
This situation put the spark up the CEO's butt, "DADDY BIG BUCKS" to

constantly get on Jim's back. "Your name sucks" - "It's worth nothing" – "Where is all the big name endorsers you said you had?" - the barrage of insults never seemed to end. On this particular day at the NAMM SHOW I guess he had enough. Daddy Big Bucks came running up to me all out of breath saying "He's after me and he has a KNIFE." He said "I'm GONNA STICK YOU," "You NAZI." The whole thing was very BIZARRE. Finally Jim appeared and Daddy Big Bucks stood behind me, acting like he was so afraid< I wanted to laugh, but I didn't. I really felt sorry for Jim. He was sick a long time with some kind of illness that made him take seizures. All this was causing him to get nasty with everyone. He told me that he took out his knife and called him a Nazi. He said he told him he wanted out and wanted his name back. This set the tone for a terrible week in Germany. Eventually he got his lawyer and started proceedings for his NAME to be returned to him. He lost his name in the court proceedings. Jim told me "YOUR NEXT, DAN", "He'll start with you next. He wants everything for himself" he was right. I was sixty four at the time and had a very serious family problem so I retired. I had it with all these people who didn't belong in the MUSIC business. Working for the GRETSCH Guitar Company was by far the best job.

THESE ARE THE GUITAR STRING WINDING MACHINES ANTO-
NIO, HIS SON AND I BUILT WHEN WE STARTED OUR OWN COM-
PANY. I DRILLED MILES OF HOLES THROUGH ROUND ALUMINUM
MATERIAL . SOME ARE STACKED ON A BENCH IN THE TOP LEFT OF
THE PICTURE. IN THE BACK YOU CAN SEE THE MILLING MACHINE
– DRILL PRESS AND LATHE USED TO MAKE THE MACHINES. I ALSO
TURNED BLUE FROM HEAD TO TOE WHEN WE USED CANS OF BLUE
METALLIC SPRAY PAINT. AFTER ALL "I'M JUST A GUITAR PLAYER" I
ALWAYS USED THIS EXCUSE WHEN I SCREWED UP.

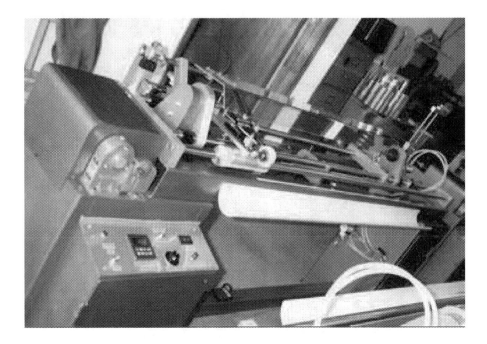

THIS IS A CLOSEUP PICTURE OF THE GUITAR STRING WIND-ING MACHINE WE MADE. IT'S METALLIC BLUE COLOR MADE THEM THE BEST LOOKING MACHINES ANTONIO EVER MADE. (with my help) IF YOU LOOK CLOSE YOU CAN SEE A HEX CORE WIRE IN THE MACHINE READY FOR THE WRAP WIRE TO BE WOUND ON TOP. THE BALL END OF THE HEX WIRE IS PLACED ON THE HOOK AT ONE END AND THE PLAIN END IS PUT IN THE OPEN CHUCK AT THE OTHER END. THE PEDAL ON THE FLOOR IS PRESSED AND THE CHUCK CLOSES AND PULLS THE CORE WIRE TIGHT BETWEEN BOTH ENDS. THE WRAP WIRE IS ATTACHED AT THE BALLEND. THE MACHINE IS STARTED, THE CORE WIRE SPINS PULLING THE WRAP

WIRE THROUGH THE TENSIONING DEVICE THAT IS PRESET. THE
LENGTH OF THE WRAP IS ALSO PRESET AT THE COMPUTER. WHEN
THAT LENGTH IS REACHED THE MACHINE AUTOMATICALLY STOPS.
THE WRAP WIRE CUTS AND THE STRING IS DONE. THE TENSION IS
VERY IMPORTANT TO THE QUALITY OF THE STRING. INTONATION,
BRILLANCE, SUSTAIN, DURABILITY AND ALL OTHER ASPECTS OF A
GOOD GUITAR STRING ARE THE RESULT OF A GOOD TENSIONING
DEVICE. ANOTHER PART OF THE MACHINE THAT IS MOST IMPOR-
TANT IS THE "CARRIAGE". THIS DEVICE CARRIES THE WRAP WIRE
ALONG SIDE THE SPINNING CORE WIRE AS IT PULLS THE WIRE
THROUGH THE TENSIONING DEVICE. ONE PERSON OPERATES
TWO MACHINES. THE MACHINE OPERATOR STANDS IN BETWEEN
TWO MACHINES AND WHILE ONE MACHINE IS WINDING A STRING
THEY START THE PROCEDURE ON THE OTHER MACHINE. THEY
CAN MAKE BETWEEN 8 AND 12 GROSS (SOMETIMES MORE) AC-
CORDING TO THE GAUGE OF THE STRING.

Dan Duffy

THIS IS THE BALLEND MACHINE

THIS MACHINE PUTS THE BALL END ON THE ROUND WIRE FOR THE PLAIN STRINGS AND THE HEX WIRE FOR THE WRAPPED STRINGS. THE WIRE IS FED AUTOMATICALLY THROUGH THE 4 WHEELS ON THE LEFT TO THE CHUCK THAT HOLDS THE BALL IN PLACE. THE CHUCK SPINS WRAPPING THE WIRE ON IT.

IT CUTS THE LENGTH AUTOMATICALLY AND DROPS THE FIN-
ISHED PRODUCT INTO THE STRING CATCH BELOW. IT IS IDEAL TO
HAVE TWO OF THESE MACHINES. ONE FOR HEX AND THE OTHER
FOR ROUND WIRE. I SPENT 40 YEARS IN THE MUSIC MANUFAC-
TURING BUSINESS , GUITARS , SERVICING IMPORTED GUITARS
AND MAKING GUITAR AND BASS STRINGS. THE BEST TIME OF IT
ALL WAS AT NIGHT ON THE BANDSTAND PLAYING MY GRETSCH
COUNTRY CLUB GUITAR.

"THE ABSOLUTE END"

Dan Duffy
Gretsch Guitars
1957 - 1970

Printed in the United States
By Bookmasters